Female Executive Stress Syndrome

The Working Woman's Guide to a Balanced *and* Successful Life

by

Sylvia Gearing, Ph.D.

THE SUMMIT GROUP • FORT WORTH, TEXAS

This book is not intended to be a substitute for professional medical or psychological advice. The reader should regularly consult a physician regarding any matter concerning her health, especially in regard to any symptoms that might require diagnosis or medical attention. Psychology is an ever-changing field. Every effort was made to ensure that the information contained in this book was the most accurate and current at the time of publication. No actual patient names are used to protect the confidentiality of the women whose lives form the basis of this story.

THE SUMMIT GROUP
1227 West Magnolia, Suite 500, Fort Worth, Texas 76104

Printed in the United States of America

1994 1995 1996 1997 1998   5 4 3 2 1

Library of Congress Cataloging-in-Publication Data

Gearing, Sylvia, 1954-
    Female executive stress syndrome: the working woman's guide to a balanced and successful life / by Sylvia Gearing.
    p. cm.
    Includes index.
    ISBN 1-56530-144-7: $24.95
    1. Women executives—Job stress—United States. 2. Women executives—United States—Psychology. 3. Stress management—United States. I. Title. II. Title: FESS.
HD6054.4.U6G43 1994
658.4'09'082—dc20
                                                        94-38324
                                                        CIP

Book design by David Sims

DEDICATION

This book is dedicated to the many remarkable women in
my private practice who prompted me to undertake this
project, and to those participants in the FESS study whose
struggles and successes are shared in these pages.

TABLE OF CONTENTS

❖

FOREWORD

Female Executive Stress Syndrome: The Working Woman's Guide to a Balanced and Successful Life, is an important and long-awaited resource for all working women who strive to lead full, happy, healthy lives. The findings of Sylvia Gearing's national study of female executives will help *all* women who search for balance between career and personal demands, and who every day struggle with the dichotomous challenges of child care and the corporate boardroom.

Until now, little attention has been given to the stress faced by working women in corporate America. The unique stress they face as women in a still primarily male bastion has been largely unexplored. As the founder of the Susan G. Komen Foundation, I am all too familiar with the lack of research dollars for women's health issues. After spending virtually all of my time on breast cancer issues for the last fifteen years, alongside other activist women, we have finally begun to convince the public and the Congress of the United States to begin to appropriate more funding for women's health issues. The Komen Foundation was one of the pioneers in this effort and has raised more than $25 million privately, making it one of the largest grantors of breast cancer research funds in the country.

This book provides landmark insight into a heretofore under-researched subject area that will help not only women at the top, but those who want to be there. It goes beyond explaining this serious stress syndrome, concentrating on solutions and strategies for success. It also offers numerous "case studies" that illustrate the particular circumstances and problems faced by women who have counseled with Dr. Gearing. Their stories are certainly illuminating, offering empathy to working women everywhere. Like the efforts of the Komen Foundation, this book is an effort produced "by women, for women." Sylvia Gearing is not a radical feminist, but a strong, central voice of reason—an advocate of a new feminism that speaks to us all.

Gearing's definition of feminism is her own:

"A vital part of the new feminism is the emphasis on a pro-woman stance that is far from the old adversarial, anti-male position that many people still associate with feminism. This new pro-women perspective emphasizes cooperation with males that enables women to augment collective efforts by providing feminine strengths that complement male strengths. Powerful women want to come together with men in a manner that acknowledges and accepts their femininity, and they are increasingly willing to do so with men who are able to collaborate in a constructive and healthy manner. These new efforts are producing increased collective strength among women that is already redefining the American workplace and will be a catalyst for real change."

As an employer and executive, I know that *Female Executive Stress Syndrome* can be a guide to change for all companies wanting to embrace diversity in the workplace as a strength that will enhance America's productivity. This book, which includes a groundbreaking, statistical study of women executives, will help us enter the new millennium with greater knowledge and understanding of the way the world should work.

—NANCY BRINKER
Founding Chairman,
Susan G. Komen Breast Cancer Foundation

PREFACE

This book is based upon a research study that was conducted by me and my husband Milt Gearing in the summer of 1994 with eighty-seven female executives across the country. Many books in this "self-help" or "pop psychology" genre claim to have conducted "research studies" that form the basis of the books, but a closer look often reveals those studies were simply informal surveys. There's nothing particularly wrong with that, except that you cannot extrapolate information from an informal survey and apply it to an entire group or population.

Several of these books fail to describe how their samples were chosen. Others appear to have utilized personal contacts with friends, business associates, or other acquaintances. In these situations, no confidentiality exists between subject and interviewer, which greatly affects what's said and how it's interpreted.

The reason psychologists and other researchers use scientific research methodology to identify and study a representative sample, as we did here, is to obtain valid and reliable results for a group that is representative of the population being studied—in our case, female executives. The women in our study didn't know us, never met us, and never will. This confidentiality and anonymity freed them to share their knowledge and feelings. I did interview thirty-six subjects over the telephone who indicated in their study packets their willingness to do a phone interview with the understanding that their identities would be protected.

As a result of our careful selection and analysis, I believe we have gathered a far more representative sample of the population than has been examined in many of the books that have come before this one. We went to great lengths to protect the integrity of this research because I believed vehemently in the importance of the questions we were asking and the answers we would receive.

ACKNOWLEDGMENTS

This book would never have been written if not for the incredible and talented women who have been my patients. I am fortunate to have been carefully "schooled" by their perceptiveness, observations, and reflections. Their contemplations have stirred my own and have forced me to grow and develop as they did. I hope this book is a tribute to what they have taught me and the struggles we resolved together.

I want to acknowledge the authors who have helped to shape my thinking in preparing this book. They include: Naomi Wolf, Susan Faludi, Gloria Steinem, Dawn-Marie Driscoll, Carol Goldberg, Arlie Hochschild, Anita Hill, and Sherrye Henry. They are wonderful teachers.

The research and teaching of Dr. James Masterson and Dr. Ralph Klein helped build my philosophy as a psychologist. They provided a window of understanding of executive women and their struggles that has been invaluable to my work.

Brian Weiss, M.D., my teacher, was helpful in explaining the publishing world and citing my own destiny as a teacher. Bill Swicegood, M.D., has been a confidante, friend, and fellow author whose conversations helped sustain my own publishing dreams. Arlene Jacobs, M.D., offered a priceless role model for me of a successful woman—physician, wife, mother.

I wish to thank Mary Rostad, the division vice-president and assistant director of personnel at JCPenney, and Diane Pearson for helping me organize the study on which this book is based.

Laine Medina has been a light in the dark for this project. Two years ago, as the FESS idea was simmering, she pushed me forward to action.

Chris and Mira Jones shared a wonderful dialogue about gender differences and the corporate world as this book was written. Their friendship provided a forum to debate new ideas and concepts.

The Summit Group's firm belief in this project never wavered. They have been helpful every step of the way. Mark Hulme, Mike Towle, Liz Bell, and Jeanne Warren helped make this project possible.

My assistant, Kay Oliver, was a tremendous support throughout the FESS study and on to deadline. Also, many thanks to Dr. Tom Carmody for his invaluable computer expertise and statistical knowledge in helping us prepare the data for this book.

Sally Giddens Stephenson has been an able and ardent supporter from the beginning. Her writing skills and careful collaboration in this project were invaluable and her feminist perspective was extremely helpful at key times. The discussions between Milt, myself, and Sally were illuminating and fast paced. Her focused and analytical thinking helped us sharpen our language and scrutinize our results.

My friend Shay Eastham told me years ago that I would write a book. Although her idea seemed ridiculous to me at the time, I have come to understand what she meant. Her dogged-ness, honesty, and support along the way helped bring this book to fruition.

My mother, Ruth Anderson Scott, has been a wonderful sounding board and kind listener. Thank you for introducing me to feminism and encouraging my self-confidence and independence when I was young. Our sons, Charlie and Chris, deserve an extra hug for putting up with all the weekends we worked on the book. I hope this study will contribute to a world that offers them, their future wives, sons, and daughters unlimited opportunities based on fairness and equality.

Enormous credit for this book goes to my husband, Milt Gearing. We always have worked well together, and this book was no exception. Milt's belief in and support of me was, as usual, solid and continuous. His research and statistical skills were instrumental in shaping our final conclusions. His deter-mined devotion to the truth steered us in the right direction. To the man I have always loved and the many other contribu-tors mentioned here, heartfelt thanks.

INTRODUCTION

She's a Tiger Lady. Diane Keaton's character in the movie *Baby Boom*. A successful businesswoman who goes after every deal with a voracious appetite. She's highly efficient, bottom-line oriented, to-the-point. Her office dress and behavior belie her gender, the identity of her role models undeniable— all men. She's followed their pin-striped, buttoned-up examples on her way up the corporate ladder.

Now that she's at the top, or near it, she finds that, outside of the office she controls so well, the rest of her world is falling apart.

Now that she's at the top, or near it, she finds that, outside of the office she controls so well, the rest of her world is falling apart. Her relationships aren't working. She's had multiple marriages, a series of short-lived affairs, or her present marriage or relationship is stagnant. Often, she's concentrated so hard on work, she finds herself alone, lonely, and depressed without any close friends. She's expected to have a career and a family, a big salary, and a well-kept house, but when the stress, depression, and burnout so carefully held at bay take over, she loses everything—she loses herself.

As a clinical psychologist who has devoted more than ten years solely to women's issues, I know this woman well. She is my typical client: a successful executive who no one would ever expect to have problems.

After graduating from Duke University and completing my Ph.D. at the University of Texas Health Science Center, I began my work in psychology at the Plano Child Guidance Center in Plano, Texas. There I quickly learned that to be effective in helping children, I had to be able to work with their mothers. My chief professional interest soon became the working woman and her psychological coping strategies. I wanted to know everything about her—what she dreamed about, how she viewed her life, how she coped successfully in a man's world. I longed to understand the psychological makeup of America's female executive. If she could compete and even flourish, how did she do it? Perhaps she could educate all of us—housewives, lawyers, waitresses, teachers, sales clerks—about survival skills for women in the nineties.

> Women succeeding in a man's world had to work twice as hard. They couldn't just be good, they had to be extraordinary.

For years these women had remained detached from their emotions to operate like the males around them in business. Women succeeding in a man's world had to work twice as hard. They couldn't just be good, they had to be extraordinary. This huge detachment defense that served them so well in business led them down a dangerous road psychologically, allowing them to avoid problems until they were acute. One morning they would wake up terribly depressed and not know why. They had fallen down a dark hole and couldn't find the exit.

Once they felt safe with me and with therapy, however, the clear thinking that ruled their careers helped them make amazingly quick progress in therapy. We would successfully blend the forgotten feminine nurturing side with the masculine driven side, and they would become more flexible, less stressed—and happy. In therapy, I would help them validate and acknowledge the feelings they had denied for so long, the feelings they weren't allowed to bring to work for fear of being called soft, a bitch, mothering, or any other label they identified as "feminine."

As they made progress, their wardrobes would change. They would choose more vibrant colors or a softer silhouette. After years of suppressing their emotions, which was both stifling and draining, a newfound femininity gave way to spontaneity and creativity they had never known—and a different kind of power born of freedom.

Their progress in therapy was mirrored by an increase in political acumen and greater accuracy of business decisions. Along with their briefcases, these women began to bring their intuitive abilities into the boardroom. As a result, their business successes flourished. They found that being female was a definite asset. Forfeiting their femininity had made them feel only momentarily comfortable in the patriarchal system, but the price they had paid was huge. Being a woman, they learned, could be synonymous with power, eloquence, and authority.

Fairly early, I began to notice striking similarities between these successful executive patients, which led me to identify a common syndrome that I call Female Executive Stress Syndrome, or FESS. Even though I first identified this syndrome among female executives, be assured that FESS applies to *all* working women. FESS is a different kind of stress than that suffered by male executives, and it's a different type of stress than that faced by women who do not work outside the home. It is unique to those courageous women who struggle to get to the top in a man's world. But it is likely to affect women well in advance of their climb to the top rung. Therefore, all women in the workforce should be advised of the symptoms that accompany FESS.

Women who have FESS are identified by a group of eight common characteristics:

1. **Perfectionism**

   I call this the "I am what I do" syndrome and it is present in virtually every executive client I see. These women expect the best—from themselves and from everyone around them. They often lose patience with others or disrespect co-workers whose work ethic doesn't measure up to their own. They measure their worth solely on the merit of their last success.

2. **Can't Take A Compliment**

   This is a simple way of expressing what can be a very complicated self-esteem problem. Women who suffer from FESS have an inability to fully integrate positive feedback. The FESS woman cannot intellectually or emotionally acknowledge that she has done something well. Often, if the FESS woman receives a compliment, she has enormous difficulty feeling it is genuine.

3. **They Would Rather Be At Work**

   For the FESS victim, working and performing are far more comfortable than relaxing. The FESS woman approaches her leisure time in the same driven, organized way she approaches work. If she plans a trip to Europe, her pre-vacation research would be extensive and probably alphabetized or contained on a laptop computer for easy access. As one FESS executive commented, "I can't just sit still. I don't want to go some place and just stay there. It would feel like an unplanned black hole of time. I have to have an objective for everything or I'm lost."

Time with her kids is also more often a structured educational activity, rather than time off to hang around the house together or watch the sun set. She may feel uncomfortable with spontaneous intimacy. These women feel the need to quantify their leisure time in the same bottom-line way they do their work time—at the end of the vacation—at the end of each day—they want to have something to show for it.

4. Split Personality

The FESS woman's personal relationships range from mildly disturbed to highly destructive and chaotic. Sometimes she becomes a dictator with her family and friends; she can't adapt from her work setting and is overly assertive in the personal realm. She simply can't turn it off at home. As one client said, "I'm so good at what I do, but I've sabotaged every relationship I've ever had." On the other hand, there quite often is a strong dichotomy between the personal and the professional sides of a woman with FESS. She may turn into a doormat when she's away from work, becoming passive and overly accommodating. It is truly amazing to see dynamic, forceful women surrender their power in this way. They suffer untold humiliations in these relationships that they would never dream of tolerating in their professional lives. Another client remarked, "My boss would fire me if I ran my department the way I run my relationships. . . . It wouldn't even be close."

5. Can't Think Pink

FESS women feel cut off from their feminine side to the point that they view femininity in a negative light and avoid any expressions that might be viewed as peculiarly feminine. They strongly identify with masculine characteristics. They don't want to be soft or feminine for fear of losing their edge. If they do not maintain 100 percent ironclad control over their lives, they feel helpless. The vast majority identify with their fathers rather than their mothers. They think their mothers are passive or unavailable or just uninteresting. They often have more male friends than female friends. As one of them put it: "I'm just not interested in talking about kids and recipes." This is how many of them view other women—as not having anything to say that would interest them.

6. Work As Escape

FESS women find solace in their work and often use work as an escape to soothe self-doubts and anxieties. They think if they will just work harder, everything will get better and the problems at home will go away. Many FESS women get a thrill from their isolation. As one bright FESS executive said, "I never fail to receive a rush when I'm the last one out of the office." Another rising executive reflected, "I find it tremendously soothing to savor the city nightscape alone in my office. I'm completely safe where no one can touch me."

7. **Performance Equals Love**

The FESS woman's relationship with her parents was often performance driven. While she was growing up, love was not unconditional. As an adult, the FESS woman measures her self-worth by what she produces at work. She has enormous difficulty unconditionally acknowledging herself. To be okay, she must be perfect.

8. **Fear Of Intimacy**

The FESS woman's intimate relationships with spouses, friends, and children are fraught with difficulties. FESS women find intimacy difficult because of the lack of structure in personal relationships. Rules within the workplace clearly structure professional behavior. With personal relationships, there are no rules or boundaries, making it harder to know how to act and how to feel. FESS women often have marriages with no real intimacy, or affairs that are cut off when they get too close.

FESS women have a preoccupation with control. As has been pointed out, FESS women may become controlling of their partners and friends at times. While this characteristic is certainly present in many of these women, it is not present in them all. What is pervasive among FESS women, though, is the need to control themselves above all else. I am convinced this control functions as a protective barrier that helps them feel less vulnerable.

Each of these eight characteristics will be explained in detail in chapter 5 ("Are You a Victim of FESS?").

After I began to identify this syndrome, I was anxious to validate it with a national study, which brings me to the origins of this book. This book has two purposes: to educate career women about Female Executive Stress Syndrome and to help women handle their lives more productively. This book draws not only upon the many experiences in my private practice that led me to identify FESS, but also upon the findings of an important national research study of eighty-seven female executives.

> This book has two purposes: to educate career women about Female Executive Stress Syndrome and to help women handle their lives more productively.

The FESS Study was designed by me and my husband, Dr. Milt Gearing, a clinical psychologist, after many hours of discussion and research. I thought of all the clients I had seen over the years and wrote down adjectives describing them and the conflicts they faced. From this list, we wrote a FESS Questionnaire that addressed all of their common characteristics and problems. (The FESS Questionnaire and a guide for self-scoring are included in the first appendix.)

The battery of psychological tests was mailed to three hundred women, a random sampling of executives from a national retailing firm, a national brokerage firm, and members of the National Association of Female Executives. After two months, nearly 30 percent of the women had completed and returned the study. A total of eighty-seven adult female respondents make up the study base for this book. All participation was completely anonymous and voluntary.

Participants completed the FESS Study Information Sheet and a FESS Questionnaire written by my husband and me to measure the type and degree of stress; a Coopersmith Self-Esteem Inventory, which measures how they feel about themselves; a Ways of Coping Questionnaire and a Coping Resources Inventory that measure both generally employed coping resources as well as specific types of coping strategies; a Profile of Mood States, which measures tension, depression, anger, vigor, fatigue, and confusion; a Jenkins Activity Survey, which measures for Type A, driven behavior; and a Bem Sex-Role Inventory, which measures for feminine, masculine, androgynous, and undifferentiated identities. (A table with more detailed descriptions of each of these instruments can be found in appendix 2.)

These various tools were chosen to provide not only a psychological profile of the participants, but also specific strategies for coping with the type of stress female executives face. A full discussion of the study and its results is in chapter 6, and appendices 2 and 3.

As the FESS study packets began to come back to our office, I called thirty-six study participants, who indicated a willingness to be interviewed for the book, and gathered a wealth of information about stress factors and coping strategies. These interviews were invaluable, blunt, and intense. Our interviewees had thought through the issues. Their observations helped form the heart of the book. Our eighty-seven study participants not only validated the existence of the Female Executive Stress Syndrome, but, more importantly, their responses helped me design a successful framework for solving their unique stress problems. This book then, in many ways, is a handbook for working women that tells how to beat the system that is stacked up against them.

Perhaps most importantly, this work points to myriad changes needed in corporate America. If the women in this study are a true indication of the top echelon of corporate America, and I believe they are, then despite the "You've Come A Long Way, Baby" ads, we haven't. We are still living and working in a patriarchy that makes the corporate ladder a difficult and unfriendly climb for women.

The good news is that, while executive women are not sharing the reins of power with their male colleagues, they are flourishing. Many women we tested are strong and powerful and determined to excel despite the odds. These women, through years of experience, have discovered specific secrets for coping in the corporate world with its enormous barriers. I want all working women to have these coping skills; they deserve them, and my research can help many working women obtain them.

Necessary changes won't take place until there are healthy women at the top, serving as role models and showing women and men on their way up that it's okay to be a truly "female" executive. I hope this book can be a first step for many women toward significant change and empowerment.

CHAPTER 1

The Changing Face
of the
American Woman

*I*N THE FORTIES, as men went off to war, seven million women entered the workforce as worker bees. Rosie the Riveter punched in at 8:00 A.M. and out at 5:00 P.M. Overnight, as Watkins, Rueda, and Rodriguez documented in *Introducing Feminism*, the government found money for day-care centers and nurseries. In her book, *Women Have Always Worked*, Alice Kessler-Harris noted that "women were offered shopping facilities, hot lunches, convenient banking arrangements, and sometimes even laundry services. Hours shrank, shifts were rearranged, new machinery was developed to take the weight off 'heavy jobs.' To encourage women to stay at work, factories set up special training programs and assigned personnel to help deal with family problems."

Rosie and the millions like her may have helped win the war, but they didn't make many decisions at the plant. Those jobs, with few exceptions, were reserved for men. Rosie's roles were well defined: she took orders, did her job, and then went home to cook, clean, and care for her family. Rosie didn't challenge the structure that defined her in such narrow terms. She had plenty of support and reinforcement along the way as she kept her nose clean, her mouth shut, and her line moving—all in the name of freedom. As Kessler-Harris noted, "For a brief two-year period, women worked in shipyards, steel mills, and ammunition factories. They welded, dug ditches, and operated forklift trucks." And when the war was over and the men returned home to claim those seven million jobs, four out of five women wanted to keep them.

> Fifty years later, Rosie runs the show, and she no longer has time to chat at the water cooler.

But fifty years later, Rosie runs the show, and she no longer has time to chat at the watercooler. Her job requires her to make important decisions daily. In addition to her official company duties, she may be expected to serve on a number of special committees as her company's "trophy" female executive. She is precise, organized, and driven to succeed. And unlike the Rosie of the forties, she no longer has the cheers of support from church and country behind her.

Is she a feminist? If you ask her, she'll say no. She may believe in equal pay for equal work. She may believe that women have the right to control their reproductive processes. She may believe that discrimination based on sex needs to stop. She may believe many of the things that feminists in the sixties and seventies fought for, but she does not identify with the image of the radical feminist created by the media.

Executive women
and the feminist backlash

SUSAN FALUDI, in her groundbreaking work *Backlash*, describes the media exclusion and distortion of productive feminist efforts. She rightly asserts that this distortion is a predictable male reaction to true progress on the part of women. She says that "a backlash against women's rights is nothing new in American history. Indeed it's a recurring phenomenon; it returns every time women began to make some headway toward equality, a seemingly inevitable early frost to the culture's brief flowering of feminism."

Faludi exposes the systematic undermining of feminism by the press, politicians, the movie and television industries, and the fundamentalist religious movements. Their twisting of the true status of women is based, again and again, on fear. They derive conclusions from personal opinions without the benefit of statistical data. Most of their assertions are simply fantasy. When pressed for data to back up their statements, they present only circular arguments.

Faludi notes that the press, "carried by tides it rarely fathoms, acted as a force that swept the general public, powerfully shaping the way people would think and talk about the feminist legacy and the ailments it supposedly inflicted on women." She adds that the press coined such popular terms as "the man shortage," the "biological clock," the "mommy track," and "post feminism." And the press was the first to "set forth and solve for a mainstream audience the paradox in women's lives. The paradox that would become so central to the backlash:

women have achieved so much yet feel so dissatisfied, it must be feminism's achievements, not society's resistance to these partial achievements, that is causing women all this pain."

The male-dominated press focused on half-truths, herding women back to traditional roles. Antifeminism is a worldwide phenomenon that is especially pronounced in American culture. Faludi notes, "In a nation where class distinctions are weak, or at least submerged, maybe it's little wonder that gender status is more highly prized and hotly defended. If the American male can claim no ancestral coat of arms on which to elevate himself from the masses, perhaps he can fashion his sex into a sort of pedigree."

It is fascinating that American sexism has thrived with such remarkable longevity. Limiting the opportunities of over half of our population is a contradiction of every democratic principle. Sexist attitudes, like racial prejudice, seek to devalue and discredit the object of disdain. There is no ambivalence in its goal.

Executive women have been struggling against the tide of male opposition and a lack of popular societal support in the American patriarchy for more than thirty years. Those who succeeded did it on their own.

While many of the executives interviewed for this book have distanced themselves from verbal identification with feminism, they embrace the cornerstone tenets of its philosophy. They have integrated feminist thinking into their everyday lives.

"I've never really cared for the term 'feminist,'" says one female executive who participated in the FESS study. "I suspect that by definition I probably am, but the term has always been sort of derogatory to me, bringing to mind sort of screaming, irrational kinds of people. Militant, nonproductive."

Yet, in the next breath, she admits that as a working woman, her life exemplifies what "feminist" stands for. Today's female executives live the philosophy of feminism, but are ambivalent about the media imaging of the label. "I just wanted to do what I wanted to do and be given a fair chance to do it," says one executive. "But I didn't think of it as feminism."

> Today's female executives live the philosophy of feminism, but are ambivalent about the media imaging of the label.

The making of survivors

FEMALE EXECUTIVES ARE, by definition, survivors. At best, they perform in a neutral work environment. At worst, their corporations undermine their achievements and chronically penalize them for their gender. While a 1993 study by Carol Scornical, the Wisconsin secretary of industry, demonstrates an increase in women executives in that state (18 percent are white women while 80 percent are white men), women still fall into the lowest-paid categories. Maggie Mahar writes about the study in the July 1994 issue of *Working Woman*: "There are many more men at the higher-earning levels; they outnumber women 3.4 to one in the $52,000 to $78,000 mark."

Executive women believe in equality on the pay scale, but despite their advances, are still far from the true power and financial rewards accorded their male peers. The glass ceiling is tragically undisturbed and very much in place.

In the fifties, when many of these executive women were children, women's roles were as clearly defined as June Cleaver's lipstick. One income sufficed for most families. The man took on the role of provider while the woman became the caretaker. As they grew up, the daughters of the fifties watched as father after father divorced the stay-at-home mom and moved on to a younger wife. My parents called it "outgrowing." The fifties were not a celebration of femininity but a constriction of it. Not allowed to grow and develop as people, these wives watched as their husbands outgrew them. Other men, identifying heavily with the American concept of disposable wives in midlife, replaced the old wife with a newer, "improved" version. The media concept of a midlife crisis seemed to apply almost exclusively to men. Clearly, as women aged, their value plummeted. Their daughters, not surprisingly, turned their backs on a lifestyle they viewed as painful and potentially risky. They vowed never to marry a man just for security.

They compared their fathers' lives to their mothers' and decided they'd rather have what their fathers had. Almost universally, executive women identified with their fathers as they grew up. Those who did identify with their mothers, did so only if their mothers were very assertive role models.

"I was very, very close to my father. I was probably the closest he came to having a son, and I think that had a lot to do with my professional orientation," says one executive who chose a male-dominated field. "I remember growing up, my father didn't read me stories at night. He told me how things worked."

"My father was terribly supportive of women," says another executive. "I was his only child for seven years. He was a geological engineer. He took me out often on his sites with him when I was five and six years old. He sort of included me, and I think it gave me some self-confidence that I could be part of a male world."

The role of militant feminism

IN THE SIXTIES AND SEVENTIES, in reaction to strict definitions of what was feminine, the pendulum swung far to the opposite side and the militant feminist movement was born.

Journalist Betty Friedan's book, *The Feminine Mystique*, set the pace. The National Organization of Women (NOW) was formed, and women began to lobby and fight discrimination. Naomi Wolf, in *Fire with Fire*, calls this era of militant feminism "victim feminism" and eloquently explains the alienation women have felt from feminism. She acknowledges "that the number of women willing to identify themselves with the word 'feminist' slipped steadily throughout the eighties even as support for women's rights steadily rose." She adds that about twice as many women believe in the goals of the women's movement as are willing to use the word "feminist."

Wolf is not willing to attribute feminism's lack of popular appeal solely to media distortion. She points out that "the reputation of feminism has become, in many places, almost indescribably rank." Tragically, she argues, female alienation from feminism is potentially self-sabotage. She says, "For just as a view of feminism divorced from women's lives is sterile, a woman's life divorced from a view of feminism she can act upon is half helpless." We found a new breed of powerful, effective, highly feminine women who were both successful and psychologically healthy. These women were unambivalent about their status and deeply invested in their personal lives. They had the best of both worlds.

Similar to other major social movements throughout the ages, the feminist movement was characterized by diversity and divisiveness. As women found their voices and joined the feminist movement, varied factions with differing opinions naturally surfaced. Given the extreme role models of the fifties, the militancy of feminism as it found its legs in the following decades was really unavoidable.

The militant feminism that thrived (while today's female executives were in college and business school) painted women as the victims of male chauvinist pigs. Such extreme images gave many mainstream women little with which to identify. In reality, many women were being victimized through job discrimination, sexual harassment, domestic violence, and rape on college campuses. But all men were not the violent, abusing brutes described by militant feminists in such black-and-white terms.

As a result, many of today's executive women, who actually share common goals with the feminist movement, turn away from it. As aggressive women, they do not identify themselves as victims. They are completely comfortable with being aggressive and competitive, having grown up with aggressive, competitive fathers as role models.

"I'm very competitive, in fact, probably competitive to a fault," says one executive. "I get a thrill out of winning, and I find a little win in every day."

"I'm getting a lot more brash," says another. "Your mother may always have told you that if you're a good little girl, good things will happen to you. Then you figure out when you're grown up that it's not necessarily the case. It's how you present to other people that has more to do with how people recognize what you do."

"I'm absolutely determined," says another executive. "I don't let anything stop me. If there's a wall, then I'll back up and figure out how to get under it or around it or over it. I'm just bound and determined."

Still another executive, describing the competitiveness she's found at the top of the corporate structure, says, "It's very hard to get in the door, but I'm a fighter, so I continue on. They can't get rid of me that quickly."

Given such statements, it's no wonder that an October 1993 denunciation of the feminist movement by Bush deputy campaign manager Mary Matalin printed in *Newsweek* struck a resonant chord with many successful female executives. Matalin's article, entitled "Stop Whining!" articulated her feelings about the "feminist fringe" fretting about oppression while mainstream women want economic equality. "Money is power. Power is equality," writes Matalin. "Feminists get a grip. . . . We are not victims; our daughters are not infants; our sons are not brutes; our men are not monstrous pigs."

While Matalin's denouncement of radical feminist thinking may have appealed to many mainstream American women, it neither acknowledges the movement's successes nor offers an alternative way to express feminist concerns. Her position also ignores the countless cases where women are truly victimized. The executive women who form the background for this book, like Matalin, cannot identify with the antimale prototypes radical feminists represent, largely because they have had to form strong alliances with men to succeed. This does not mean, however, that we have conquered all barriers; women still make less than men for the same jobs, are still victims of violence far more often than men, and are still harassed in the workplace. And, as Naomi Wolf noted, "right out of the starting gate, women's relationship to feminism was damaged by the fact that to avow feminism stood women a good chance of costing them their jobs."

As the dinosaurs of corporate America begin to die, however, and the sixty-plus men who have ruled for so long retire, there is a sense of true hope that the corporate ranks will change and that harassment will become a thing of the past as women gain power.

As the dinosaurs of corporate America begin to die, however, and the sixty-plus men who have ruled for so long retire, there is a sense of true hope that the corporate ranks will change and that harassment will become a thing of the past as women gain power.

Says one female executive: "As some of these folks, men—because there aren't that many women—in their early sixties are retiring or dying or whatever the case may be, and we are coming into positions of leadership and of power that will have a lot to do, I think, with the changes. At least the changes that I see coming forward in our workplace."

The search for acceptance

FEMALE EXECUTIVES have an understandable desire for acceptance by the males in their ranks. Their mentors have been men. These women can hardly hope to get ahead while openly attacking the majority of their colleagues. They are without female peers, but still have the desire to form friendships with colleagues. What I see with female executives is an extension of a psychological transformation that has been well documented in girls going through puberty. Being unique or different is seen as undesirable, so girls try to stay within the path. A premium is placed on conforming to a certain look, a certain lifestyle, certain achievements. During puberty, girls back away from public displays of power, and from success in subjects like math and science considered male dominion. (Meanwhile, as Sadker and Sadker point out, girls educated in all female environments continue to score high in math and science throughout their education.) This twelve-year-old's early trials form the basis for later Female Executive Stress Syndrome (FESS) development:

> Katherine doesn't get it. In Milwaukee, in her private, all-girls school, she excelled—had since kindergarten. She is an achiever, and is equally interested in the sciences and humanities. Beautiful, bright, and funny, Katherine has it all. She has always been popular—until now. She thinks how happy she was before they moved to St. Louis.

Katherine experiences daily friction at her new school. The first few weeks in seventh grade are a descent into hell. The teacher announces her grades—which are invariably the highest—to chastise the rest of the class for their lack of effort. This makes Katherine want to crawl under a rock. "I'm doomed . . . doomed!" she announces to her mother one night. "None of these kids, especially the boys, like smart girls. The teacher is killing any chance I have of making friends!" Katherine starts to cry inconsolably.

To avoid more ridicule, Katherine withdraws. She is torn between her love of learning and competing against herself, and the loneliness that surrounds her life. The few other girls who are good students also live solitary lives and seem awkward and bookish. They are overly proud of their schoolwork because it is all they have. As Katherine says to her best friend, Melinda, back in Milwaukee, "There's no way I can be smart and have friends. I can't fit in because I'm labeled 'that smart girl' and no one wants to talk to me unless they want to use me to help with their homework. The only way I'll ever have a boyfriend is to act like an airhead."

Katherine's experience, unfortunately, is typical. As Myra and David Sadker found in *Failing in Fairness*, so many pitfalls surround adolescent girls: "physical vulnerability, the closing of options, the emphasis of thin, pretty, popular, the ascendancy of social success over academic achievement, the silencing of their honest feelings, the message that math and science are male domains, the short-circuiting of ability that renders them helpless, the subtle insinuations that boys are really the smart ones (they just don't try). Girls who succumb to these messages are at emotional and academic risk, in danger of losing not only their confidence and their achievement but the very essence of themselves."

Voted "Class Brain" in the eighth grade, I cried for a week. I had been assertive in class and tested consistently well, but when I was recognized for those attributes, I immediately felt unpopular and unaccepted. I vowed to change. I transformed myself in high school, dropped out of honors math, and did everything I could do to make myself into a stereotypic female. The end product of these alterations in personality was acceptance—and a destruction of my self-esteem that would take years to rebuild.

At the time, I had no female role models who demonstrated a balance between feminism and intelligence. I could be either feminine, passive, and accepted, or assertive, academically superior, and on the social fringes. I was not to threaten the stereotypes if I wanted to succeed socially. Not until I entered college was I finally able to find support for my intellect. Several of my female professors nourished my academic ability and taught me not to hide my curiosity. It had taken me years to find an atmosphere that would nurture my whole self—including that part of me that had been voted Class Brain back in the eighth grade.

As the FESS study shows, female executives also alter their identities to be accepted. They deny not only the feminist movement, but the entire feminine side of themselves to build relationships. In the sex role study we conducted, the majority of executive women rated highly masculine. They have successfully suppressed traditional feminine characteristics to blend more easily into the fabric of corporate America. Consider Dorothy, a bright young attorney who refuses to acknowledge any feminine interests or needs:

Every time Dorothy is given a deadline, she makes it. Behind her back other attorneys call her "MBH" for "most billable hours." In the two years since she graduated from Georgetown Law School, there is no doubt about it: Dorothy's billable hours are the highest in the history of the firm. Even Mr. Jasper, the sexist founder of the firm—and previous record holder—is secretly impressed. He mutters his congratulations to Dorothy at associates' meetings, though he wonders out loud how a "girl" can handle the pressure.

Dorothy isn't surprised. She just keeps working. After her parents went through a high-profile, high-society divorce when she was nine, she lived alone with her father, a federal judge, and their housekeeper, Mrs. Appleby, in a Chicago brownstone. Nobody talked to her about her feelings or even how her days had gone. Her father's priority had been to develop Dorothy's analytical thinking and reasoning skills. He wanted to make sure she didn't develop any of her mother's "bad habits"—like wanting to share experiences or spending time relaxing together. If the judge had anything to say about it, Dorothy's mind would be a highly trained and disciplined instrument, and she would eventually do grand things in the legal world. He would extend his own achievements through hers. So now, at the age of twenty-five, Dorothy has made work her world.

Cloistered in her cluttered associate's office, she has fashioned herself into a legal "machine." She rises at 5:00 A.M. and exercises vigorously—not out of vanity or concern for her health, but because the physical activity helps her focus. She arrives early at work and labors vigorously all day, without interruption. She researches each legal question, aware of her passion for the truth and her personal demand for excellence. She is certain that the law is the right choice only for those who have an utter devotion to logic, analysis, and deliberation. She is sure without that devotion all is lost. The law defines things as black or white, and so does she.

Dorothy has no personal life outside the practice of law. She is attractive and slender, and men seem to notice her even though her attire has all the flair of a nun's habit. However, Dorothy has no awareness of her sexual appeal. Dorothy lost all interest in her femininity when she lost her mother. She had no use for intuition or any other "feminine" characteristics, and viewed her sex as a liability in her practice of law; Dorothy refused to compromise her career by developing that side of herself.

Dorothy's attitude is common among FESS women. Through therapy sessions and interviews conducted for this book, it is apparent to me that exhibiting these typically "male" characteristics is a sort of corporate foray into survival of the fittest. These women have, in a sense, become men to beat a system that is stacked up against them.

The new feminist movement— finding the right balance

THE NEW FEMINIST MOVEMENT, yet to be embraced by the majority of corporate women, is not about "having it all," but about having a choice. Today's corporate society won't let anyone—male or female— have it all. You cannot be president of a Fortune 500 manufacturing company, have three well-adjusted kids with whom you are close, have an intimate relationship with your life partner, and have time for yourself to retreat and rejuvenate. This is true for anyone at the very top. However, absentee dads who are off running the world are not fraught with the same guilt that absentee moms must face.

> The new feminist movement, yet to be embraced by the majority of corporate women, is not about "having it all," but about having a choice.

Most corporations devour the time of top executives. But you can have a viable career and a happy home and family life. Unfortunately, for those at the very top, the world must change before you can have it all. (More on this subject in chapter 8.)

New feminists want freedom in their choices. They don't want to have to reject men to embrace feminism. They want a

F
E
S
S

partner and equal pay, too. We are at a crossroads now in the feminist movement and it is time to pull women back into being proud of what they innately are. One of the saddest things I see in my practice are young women right out of college who reject the feminist label. Yet they are doctors and lawyers and upcoming executives, and they are where they are because of the women's movement, because of feminists who came before them. To them and to many executive women decades older, the words feminine and feminist are tainted. Women should not have to reject their feminine side to get ahead in the corporate world. When they do, it isn't any wonder that years later it takes its toll on their self-esteem.

To fully realize our potential as women, I am convinced that we are going to have to reidentify and realign ourselves with the goals of feminism. We can be hard and driven *and* nurturing and caring. We need to develop the flexibility to change roles. The powerful woman is neither a man-hater nor an emulator of men but a whole woman.

Make no mistake—do not interpret this espousing of the "new powerful woman" as a tearing down of women today. Women have altered themselves to achieve important personal goals. Now it is time for the system to change, to be more accepting of women as they truly are. Too often, popular psychologists and the all-powerful media have said that it is women who need to change, that their problems are not a constrictive patriarchal society or corporate world but the neurosis within.

Author Susan Faludi illuminates this phenomenon in *Backlash*. Having briefly celebrated the strong women in our midst, the media spent the bulk of the eighties and all of the nineties to date telling women that what they really needed to be happy was to abandon their professional lives and embrace home and hearth. Popular psychology was a big culprit here, Faludi points out:

> To the vast female readership of self-help manuals, the advice experts delivered a one-two punch. First they knocked down the liberated woman, commanding that she surrender her "excessive" independence, a mentally unhealthy state that turned her into a voracious narcissist, a sterile cuckoo. Then, having brought the "victim" of feminism to her more feminine knees, the advice writers reaped the benefits—by nursing the backlash victim. In the first half of the eighties, the advice experts told women they suffered from bloated egos and a "fear of intimacy"; in the second half, they informed women that atrophied egos and "codependency" were now their problems. In the decade's war on women, these popular psychologists helped fire the opening shots—then rushed to the battlefield to bandage the many wounds.

I am not joining the fray of psychologists who tell women to abandon their professional achievements to nurture relationships. I am asserting that there is room in this world for a new, powerful woman. This woman is someone who uses her intuition, who understands her feelings, who is not afraid of her own power or the power of other women, who is fully self-acknowledging, who is goal-directed and driven in what she wants to accomplish but still values relationships. The powerful woman is fully sexual. She has been able psychologically and physically to explore her sexuality. If she chooses to have children, she does it in a way that compliments her life, professionally and personally.

F
E
S
S

This woman is the strength of a new feminism that does not discard "old feminism," but rather improves and remodels it to better address the needs and hopes of women in the nineties. The empowerment of women is a fresh approach to women's rights that I believe is winning a steadily increasing body of supporters. Gone are the bra-burning days where virtually all aspects of the traditional feminine role were rejected. The new powerful woman will no longer have to imitate a masculine style in an effort to conduct business, because this implies a fundamental rejection of a vital part of women's identities.

Women who have emerged from FESS find that they are better at what they do when they rely upon formerly suppressed "female" characteristics. When women give credence to their intuitive, spiritual side, the so-called "feminine" side, the side not usually seen in the business world, they are more effective at work. Without exception, when women con-strict their emotional life and ignore their feelings, they more often miscalculate business situations and misread people. The higher you are in the corporate hierarchy, the more important it is to be politically astute. You cannot afford to misjudge. If you are going to be successful and maintain executive status, you have to nurture and develop the side of yourself so often labeled female.

Women who have emerged from FESS find that they are better at what they do when they rely upon formerly suppressed "female" characteristics.

Without feeling and intuition, business decisions are con-crete, black-and-white. If you continue to see work as a series of tasks to be completed rather than as a series of lessons to be learned, you will eventually fail. But women executives who have learned not only to develop the concrete but also the cognitive and emotional sides of themselves find more pleasure in their work and are at less risk for burnout. The new powerful woman celebrates the feminine characteristics that make her a woman and accomplishes this by expressing feminine identities in effective approaches to accomplishing her goals.

Women who recover from FESS—and those who succeed as executives without falling prey to it—are discovering that there can be a positive "power in pink" that showcases a woman's unique strengths and abhors the use of sexual seduction in exchange for privileges and promotions. Being a woman and relying on characteristics that have traditionally been labeled "for women only" is an asset, not a liability, and women are realizing and asserting this more and more every day.

A vital part of the new feminism is the emphasis on a prowoman stance that is far from the old adversarial, antimale position that many people still associate with feminism. This new prowoman perspective emphasizes cooperation with males, enabling women to augment collective efforts by providing feminine strengths that complement male strengths. Women in authority want to work with men in a manner that acknowledges and accepts their femininity, with men who are able to collaborate in a constructive and healthy manner. The increasing collective strength of women will end the mudslinging between radical feminists and right-wing conservatives.

Under the new feminism, women will offer more support to other women. We are beginning to see this as women in corporate leadership positions act as mentors for those entering

F
E
S
S

the ranks. These new efforts are producing a level of collective strength among women that is already redefining the American workplace and will be a catalyst for real change.

One female executive describes this collective strength as the "old girls network," yet it bears little resemblance to the old boys network of golf playing, smoky bars, and country clubs.

"The 'old girls network' is very strong and alive and well," she says. "As there are more and more women, again in my organization, and I can only speak for mine, but more and more women gaining different positions of power, it grows. It's sort of like—this is going to sound kind of funny—but it's sort of like a subliminal sensing device. We kind of seek each other out and connect up either one through the other or somebody knows somebody else. It's building. It's getting there. It's very strong. The other one, the 'old boys network,' though, is there. It's never going to go away. There's a lot of time spent between those folks doing nothing but that. I guess maybe their positions and their longevity with the company enables them to have the time to do a lot of that. But there's an awful lot of time spent. They're worse than women, and we're the ones that are stereotyped that all we do is gab. But, I really feel that that's what that is. It's a stereotype. I think if the truth would really be known, that the men are worse than the women at this. I really feel that way."

Women frequently prefer female doctors, lawyers, and psychologists. Many of these professionals already enjoy unprecedented levels of respect, and I believe this will continue as the new feminism grows. Women are comfortable with these female professionals, who they feel assured will provide an optimum level of understanding and response to their needs, with a built-in guarantee that service will be provided free of any sexual discrimination or harassment.

Women are changing their own views of women in the workplace. Says one executive, "I've seen a growing support among professional women supporting each other and helping each other, an empathy. We used to—and I'm going back a number of years—almost laugh among ourselves at the times when even we would assume if we saw another woman that she was probably a clerical person. How awful that assumption was—we were doing it to ourselves."

Women are reaching out to mentor other women and are enjoying the experience. One executive who mentors a couple of women says, "I thoroughly enjoy those relationships. We have lunch quite frequently and I find that very fulfilling. It's probably one of the best things about my career."

Janet is a well-established female executive who is ready to mentor. She chooses one younger woman with whom she works closely to begin the process:

> Janet has risen through the corporate ranks like a good soldier. At fifty-two, she has seen it all—sexual harassment, discrimination, the old boys' network, that ever-present, ever-intact glass ceiling that is finally within reach. Nothing surprises her and nothing throws her. She is a pro and she knows it. Janet has made it against great odds.
>
> Frustrated with the pro-male system, she is determined to save other women the aggravation she has

experienced. Janet is ready to mentor. Her assistant, Madeleine, is bright, savvy, and ready to learn—the perfect candidate.

Janet wants to guide Madeleine past the pitfalls and over the hurdles that have snagged and sabotaged so many capable women through the years. She longs to share the business insight that was so hard won. By providing that insider's knowledge, she hopes to help Madeleine achieve a level of success and avoid politically costly blunders.

Janet spends her drive time every morning mulling over this prospect. She wants her mentoring to make a difference for Madeleine. She wonders how best to distill her knowledge into workable, concrete information that other women will be able to take advantage of. Janet knows that effectiveness in business has more to do with how well you develop yourself as a person than with the number of hours you work or even the level of knowledge you possess. She embraces her own power, is fair but assertive, and uses diplomacy in interpersonal relating. She is corporate "street smart." Her intuition has held her in good stead and gotten her out of countless jams, helping her resuscitate difficult client relationships. For the last twelve years she has been the corporate wonder woman. But how best to relay this to Madeleine in a way that she can use it?

Teaching another woman makes Janet think about the strategies she employs and forces her to reexamine her own understanding of their industry. She revisits old beliefs and challenges herself to deepen her own awareness. Most importantly, she begins to teach Madeleine how to rely on her intuition and redefine herself as a strong women with power, elegance, and clout. She realizes that assisting Madeleine with her career development is also helping her to further her own growth— and she's having fun in the process.

Mentoring was a fruitful experience for Janet. She found, as do most women, that having other women to rely upon eases the frustrations of a patriarchal workplace. Women are still tired of and angry about sexual harassment, however, and fewer women are willing to put up with it in their place of employment. As sexual harassment cases flooded the courts following the Anita Hill debacle, harassment became a serious economic issue for corporations. When the bottom line is affected in corporate America, the rank and file are sure to change.

Supportive husbands are another new source of support for some executive women. If these women are happily married, they are married to men who are supportive of their careers. In her article, "Trophy Husbands," first published in *Working Woman*, journalist Nikki Finke writes about high-profile wives who have met their matches. Couples such as Jane Fonda and Ted Turner, media maven Diane Sawyer and Hollywood director Mike Nichols, and Elizabeth and Bob Dole exemplify matches that work for high-powered females. Business has a lot to do with the attraction here. Says banker Darla Moore about her real estate deal-maker husband, Richard Rainwater, "A substantial percentage of our personal conversations are business, business, business."

But whereas these great minds do think alike, there also is built-in support and understanding. Says one executive about her husband, "He's understanding and supportive. He's my best friend. We do an awful lot of sharing of work-related issues, management problems, and a lot of sharing of good and bad things that are going on in our businesses." Another executive credits her husband for helping her "keep sane" through the bar exam. "He's terrific. We've been married almost seventeen years," she says.

As the new feminism emerges, more and more women embrace a collective movement, steadily coming together in agreement about who they are, how society should treat them, and where they are headed. They also increasingly agree that the final outcome should not be women win, men lose. Life does not have to be—and, in fact, should not be—a zero-sum game. The new feminism pursues victory for all.

CHAPTER 2

◈

Life at the Top:
The Unique Stresses Faced by
Female Executives

ROM TIME IMMEMORIAL it has been said, "It is a man's world." Nowhere is this more true today than in the upper echelons of corporate America. Women first entered the workforce in droves fifty years ago. Called by their country to factories and offices to fill the void left by men summoned to war, women responded enthusiastically. They were rewarded by being told to go back to their homes once the men returned. Since that time, though women have made great strides, every woman who works knows this frustrating fact to be true: the boardroom is a patriarchy. Period.

Daily, women battle for legitimacy in the workplace, and it's an uphill fight. In many social circles, working women are frowned on, despite the undeniable economic necessity for women to work in today's economy. It seems that those most critical of working women are men who enjoy the status quo and wish to protect their monopoly on power, or women whose affluent lifestyles allow them to reap the rewards of a sexist system.

Both of these sectors seek to defend a system that benefits them as individuals, not women or society as a whole. They show neither compassion nor a clear understanding of what most women face every day of their lives in this country.

For the executive woman ambition is a double-edged sword: not only must she endure the criticism all working women face, she also must struggle with society's ambivalence about a woman with power. Strong women with clout are constant targets of our male-dominated society. Many people— both men and women—still paint women with power as unfeminine and potentially emasculating to any man within a fifty-mile radius. They try to vilify her to neutralize her. These are outdated and narrow points of view, having little to do with the way the world works in the nineties. Women are running the boardroom. They have embraced the reins of power without ambivalence. And they are having full, passionate relationships with the men they love. Nothing could be more feminine.

The consensus among women interviewed for this book is that the older white male is the most resistant to women at high levels in corporations. "Younger men either haven't been put in a corner where they're trapped and have to lash out, or they see women co-workers as team members," says one executive, adding that the older men have trouble working with women on an equal playing ground. Yet other women have seen the older patriarchs of big business lend a hand to women on the way up. "I've seen an element of primarily older men who have daughters that seem to be more supportive and understanding," says one executive. While this bequeathing of power from benevolent patriarchs is encouraging, it carries its own danger, women warn. When the patriarch and his protection are gone, so is her power.

The present study and a decade of clinical experience have shown me that working in this patriarchy creates a whole set of stress factors for female executives that male executives simply don't have to deal with. No matter what business these women are in, their worries, fears, and complaints fall into similar categories:

- They feel that because they are women, they have to give 150 percent just to hold their own with male counterparts.
- They are frustrated and resentful because they make only one-half to two-thirds the income of their male peers and because they feel limited by a glass ceiling.
- They feel cut off from the political interplay of the good old boy network.
- They are undermined by the network of women who are not part of the corporate power structure.
- They have to deal with the unfortunate reality of sexual harassment and sexism in the workplace.
- They have no role models or support system of peers.
- When they go home, more often than not, they begin a second job; whether they are married or not, most of these women are primarily responsible for home, hearth, and the health and welfare of any children.

Unlike male executives, female executives must also deal with the ongoing comparison between themselves and women who

**F
E
S
S**

have chosen to stay at home. Here, too, their stresses are unique. While studies have shown that housewives are at higher risk for depression than women who are fully employed, executive women are subject to hyper-stressful demands that set them apart and put them at risk for Female Executive Stress Syndrome (FESS).

Unlike male executives, female executives must also deal with the ongoing comparison between themselves and women who have chosen to stay at home.

Sociologists at the Wellesley Center for Research on Women at Columbia University have found that both women who are fully employed and those who are not find their family and home life the most stressful part of living, and that working outside the home may actually decrease the negative effects of stress. A Canadian study of depression led by Jay R. Turner, professor of sociology at the University of Toronto, reinforces those findings. Turner found that while women who work are subject to more stress, they are less likely to suffer from depression. These studies, however, do not focus on the women forging lonely paths to the top of corporate America. Both nonexecutive working moms and nonworking moms have significant support systems and plentiful examples of success from which to model. The media, this country's political and religious structure, and our whole social ideology all reinforce the notion that women who stay at home with their children or those working women who arrive at day care promptly at 5:00 P.M. are shining examples of motherhood. Senior female executives, who are more likely to be on an airplane at 5:00 P.M. or on another continent, rather than at home with their children,

F
E
S
S

are more likely to receive disdain than accolades for their parenting.

Following is a more comprehensive explanation of the unique stress factors that can lead to FESS, with excerpts from interviews with women who participated in the FESS study.

They feel like they have to give 150 percent

Overwhelmingly, female executives feel they have to be far better than the men around them to hold on to the positions they already have earned. They believe second chances are rare so the decisions they make must be right if they are to garner the respect of their male peers. Men can afford to make mistakes; they cannot. They get to work early and stay late and make sure every step they take is beyond reproach.

One executive interviewed for the book calls this the issue of "proof." "We have to prove that we have a brain, that we do know what we're talking about, that we're not just a piece of hair and makeup in a dress," she says.

As a result, executive women must put more background material into every presentation. Men may be able to come up with an idea and fly by the seat of their pants, she says, but women have to be a lot better prepared.

The energy expended to give more at work exacts a price at home. "A lot more women have come so far and gotten prestigious positions and have been able to pull themselves up and be considered one of the players," says this executive. "It's just what you've got to give up to get to that point—your life."

Despite the efforts of many large corporations to promote women, in upper management, says one executive with a large retailing firm, "they're still more likely to promote a man who does fairly well than a woman who does exceptional." Part of the reason for this, she says, is that most men—at least 80 percent in her estimation—have extreme difficulty in reporting to a female.

"You still get a lot of talk about how she got there. 'She blew her way to the top. Who was she sleeping with to get this job?' It's still going on. It's just not as publicized as much as it used to be," she says. "Women have a stigma. 'Well, she can't be that smart. She must have done something to get where she is.' "

And although executive women feel the need to work harder and longer and to do better, they must also work hard to keep emotions in check. Says another female executive, "I think women still have a much more difficult time of expressing themselves, of expressing anger or displeasure. They're under a lot of scrutiny about every little thing they do and how they express it. Sometimes things are read into how they handle themselves that I don't think a man would have to deal with. I'm very cautious about what I say and how I say it."

Female executives have to be far more politically savvy than males to hold their own, women say. They cannot risk being perceived as too cocky or proud of their success. Where a woman is called "cocky," a man might be called "confident." Where a woman might be called "a bitch," a man is seen as "decisive."

They make less income than their male peers

A 1992 STUDY by Korn/Ferry International and the UCLA Anderson Graduate School of Management of executive women in the largest U.S. corporations showed that salaries doubled from those recorded a decade before, from $92,000 in 1982 to an average of $187,000 in 1992. Those surveyed reported working as long as their male counterparts—at least fifty-six hours per week—yet they only made two-thirds what the men did in a Korn/Ferry study of 1989.

"The salary differential may be explained somewhat by the women's younger age (forty-four years, compared to fifty-two for the men in 1989) and by the fact that more are at the vice president level, but unequal pay is still a fact," the study concludes.

The women who participated in the FESS study agree, and they point to a number of other glaring inequalities in the workplace. One woman tells of an experience she had while at a large national accounting firm. She took over a job previously held by a man and estimates his salary was four times what she was paid when she took the job. Also, she adds, her predecessor had an assistant to help him with the workload and she did not.

"I did the job better and probably faster than he did because I had a family to support, and felt that I would be compensated eventually for it. But I was not," she says. When she finally went in for her job review, she had a figure in mind for a raise but was offered only half that amount. "When they told me that there was no way, that no one could ever get that kind of a raise, I said, 'Well, the other person, I know, was making considerably more than I was.' They said, 'Well, he has a family.' I said, 'Well, I don't exactly have chickens running around in the backyard.' "

While many of the women interviewed say that female executives are not having trouble getting promoted, they say those promotions don't come with the salaries or the clout they once held for men.

"They're elevating us," one says, "but they're not including with that elevation some of the authority and responsibility that men at comparable levels have. It's like, 'We'll put you there so you're seen, but we're not quite sure we're ready to give you the reins yet.' "

Female executives say that the glass ceiling may show some hairline fractures, but it is far from being broken. At the very top—CEO, CFO levels—the structure is firmly in place. "Just because there are token women at high positions, doesn't mean the floodgates have opened," one executive says. "I think there are a lot of women in their twenties now that don't realize that they're going to hit a glass ceiling very quickly. I think that it hasn't even entered their minds."

They are cut off from the good old boy network

AS POLITICALLY SAVVY as these women must be to succeed, eventually, they say, a door is shut in their face. Often, it is a locker room door. They still feel cut off from the informal network that works so well for male executives. The golf course, the men's lounge at the country club, the "gentlemen's clubs" where much male bonding occurs at the expense of scantily clad females, the after-work socializing that goes on between men. Without access—and invitation—to these venues, these women say they find it difficult, if not impossible, to forge the friendships and build the loyalty that often can help you get through rough times in business.

An executive with a large national corporation says she and other women executives at her company definitely feel left out of this informal network. This costs them when their male peers go looking for input on important issues at the office.

"There are just certain things we miss out on, like we're not always invited to play golf. As a result, we are not as close and it seems like they don't seem to want to hear what we say or rely on us for honesty and opinions," she says, adding that they do value the opinions of their male buddies at work.

This executive and her male boss are both going to an out-of-town conference and she says that he hasn't approached her about flying out or coming back together. "It's in California, and he has not even asked me when I'm flying out. He has not told me when he's leaving or when he's flying back. I feel like there's a level of respect there, that we should have tried to go together, and I didn't really feel like it was my responsibility to do that since he's my boss.

While many of the women interviewed say that female executives are not having trouble getting promoted, they say those promotions don't come with the salaries or the clout they once held for men.

"For the same meeting a year ago, he went with a male friend of his from our office. They flew in together and got drunk on the plane, and left together. I don't think he even realizes what he's doing," she says.

Although she claims that many women in her company can relate similar experiences, they haven't made it an issue because they are afraid it might jeopardize their positions by painting them as whining and emotional.

Another executive says that the old boy's network exists at the office as well as after hours and that she has seen it work to undermine women. "They have withheld information or have not invited me to meetings," she says. "It was awful, incredible discrimination."

They are undermined by other women at work

MANY OF THE WOMEN who participated in the FESS study say that the worst sabotage they've experienced at work was at the hands of another woman. It may be that as many women as men are uncomfortable with women in power. Part of this phenomenon can be explained by child-rearing techniques from the fifties and sixties. Women were reared to be adversaries. The basic objective was to "get a man," therefore, women looked at other women as natural competitors who were not to be trusted. Though the rules have changed, this study indicates that many women have not.

"You'd think it would be the opposite way, that we'd stick up for each other," says one executive. "But you've got most women who have gotten to a place of power and position in their organization, and they see other women coming in who are a little smarter or a little brighter, and they get very territorial. There is a power play. Most women that I've worked with in a professional manner, if they feel a little threatened, if you might know a little more than they know, they think you're out for their jobs or their territory. And then you get the same thing you get from the men—'She did this to get this position'—you get the women saying it back to the women. They're threatened. They've worked hard to get to where they are, and then here comes another woman who they feel didn't pay her dues, and they think, 'She's going to take my job, and I'm going to be out in the street.' Especially if the woman is younger."

This executive says that in her career she has experienced women creating falsehoods and making negative comments to her superiors to make her uncomfortable about her position. "I finally gave up my position and looked elsewhere. This was around six years ago. But I feel like it happened because I was smart and knowledgeable and young."

Another executive says women will take much more abuse on the job from men than they will from women. "They resent a woman boss. No matter what you do. I mean, you will discipline them and maybe you might raise your voice a little, well you get reported. I've been in this business twenty-five years, and I've been screamed at many times and never would have thought of reporting it. They don't report men. But, they're not going to take that from a woman.

"Women tend to back stab," she adds. "Men see each other's faults, but they're always buddies. But if you become a boss and you're a woman, then the women no longer trust you. They think you're going to go do something, and you're going to ruin their life. So they go crying to somebody else that you're being cruel."

One woman, who is a senior legal counsel, says her company, perhaps unwittingly, creates adversarial situations with its female executives. "I think because the company is pushing and promoting women and trying to make them very visible so that everyone knows that it's doing these great things tends to pit us against each other. The company wants people on certain task forces or nominated to a certain important committee, and it usually comes down to two or three women candidates. It can get very competitive. Sometimes you sit back and it starts eating at you a little bit."

They must deal with sexual harassment and sexism

SEXISM AND SEXUAL HARASSMENT in the workplace are alive and well in the 1990s, say the executives in the FESS study. "It's still the same as it was twenty years ago, it's just a little fluffier now," says one. Virtually all of the women interviewed for this book had experienced some form of sexual harassment or sexism at the office; however, they also had developed a thick skin and did not find such behavior an insurmountable barrier.

The Korn/Ferry International-UCLA Anderson Graduate School of Management study seconds our findings. In that study, 27 percent of the women reported sexism as the greatest obstacle to their success in 1992 as compared to 39 percent in 1982; however, as many as 59 percent said they had experienced sexual harassment. Fourteen percent of these women reported the incident to a supervisor; another 37 percent confronted the harasser privately.

Although our study respondents have found ways to cope with these stresses, they continue to be great sources of frustration.

"I've had lewd comments, touching. I received a birthday kiss once from a gentleman I was working with, and he decided to shove his tongue down my throat. You always run into instances of it. I'm an easygoing person. I get along well with everybody and depending on the people you work with, there is a certain amount of flirtation that goes on. But, you know, it keeps things light in the area to tell dirty jokes every now and then. You have to work with these people. They have to be able to relate to you as they would another man," says one executive. She reports experiencing harassment that has "crossed the line" three times in her career.

"I've just kept everything between the two of us, and it gets straightened out at the point when it does cross the line. I get a little violent from time to time. If a guy shoved his tongue down my throat, he did receive a sharp punch into the stomach, yes. And he was informed that if he ever thought of doing anything like that again he would be in more severe pain," she says.

"It's a man's world. It'll always be a man's world," says another top executive for a national corporation. "We try as hard as we might, and the stigma is always the same: that the women just shouldn't be in the workplace, that they're taking jobs away from men who have families. They don't realize most of the women have families, too."

One corporate counsel for a large company says she handles harassment with humor. "I just think it's so stupid. I just laugh at it and tell them to go away if they even start. I can't take it seriously. Maybe that's my own personal attitude: 'Don't bother me, we've got a job to do. Don't be silly.' " But when it comes to sexism, her frustrations rise. "I do a lot of litigation support. I definitely feel constrained because I'm a woman in a man's world, depending on what part of the country I'm in. I travel a lot of the East Coast into the South and then out towards the Midwest and up into Canada. It depends on where I am as far as whether I'm taken seriously or not. I find in the South a lot of the 'good old boy' stuff. As I get older, I find less and less tolerance for that. I expected to have to prove myself when I was younger. Now as I'm older, and I've had more than twenty years of professional experience, and I'm an authority in my field, I find it absolutely intolerable when men ignore me because I'm a woman—and it happens.

"One particularly clear incident happened in a large southern city where I went into the company as an expert and instructor. They had serious problems, but the vice-president there could hardly give me the time of day. And I was there to help him meet his deadlines. He is still calling his women staff experts 'girls.' He wouldn't look at the documents that I'd given him. He said, 'This isn't important. I can't be bothered with this now. I have too many other things to do. You girls get on with your work.' I couldn't believe it. That was probably the worst experience I've had in a long time," she says.

Since this man was her client and she was there to support him, she couldn't very well tell him where to go. But she sure wanted to.

"Then I turned around and just hopped on a plane and went from there to San Francisco, where I was part of a collaborative meeting. I was the authority. I was one of the team. I was respected. I was treated as an equal, if not a superior. It was just the most intriguing contrast I have yet had in a short time," she says.

They have no role models or support system of peers

IT'S LONELY AT THE TOP. This is especially true for female executives who have reached the pinnacle. Their climb was a solitary one, with no other women to assist them. And by the time these women get the key to the executive washroom, those men who were their mentors most likely long since have retired. "There weren't any before me. I'm it," says one executive. She's echoed by many other women interviewed who said they were the first women to serve in their positions.

Away from work, many of these women have trouble forging friendships with other women who don't face the same daily demands on their time.

"Unfortunately, the women that have been close friends of mine, once they have children, it's not that we don't still care about each other, but we've really drifted apart," says one executive who never had children.

Another executive, who relocated with her company, says her friends are in another city at her company's headquarters, and because of her heavy travel schedule, she has found it almost impossible to keep up neighborhood friendships. "My kids are older, so I don't have those natural friendships with mothers of my children's friends," she says. "I have more male friends now. Probably because there's more opportunity for that. There are so few women where I am. And also, I find that I don't do coffee-klatsching talk very well."

These executive women feel cut off from other women altogether. As a result, when they have time to stop, they find themselves alone.

They go home to more work

AFTER TWELVE HOURS, executive women may leave their jobs, but not their responsibilities. Quite often they still are expected to be the primary caretakers at home. Since they have high incomes, they don't go home to scrub the toilets; however, the organization and care of the home, and the care for their children, still falls to them. Whereas top male executives might come home to a martini and dinner, female executives come home to deal with nanny problems, dinner planning, and maids who were no-shows for the second time in two weeks.

> After twelve hours, executive women may leave their jobs, but not their responsibilities. Quite often they still are expected to be the primary caretakers at home.

"It's like having two personalities," says one executive. She's the mother of a five-year-old and hasn't had a vacation in more than six years. "The company doesn't care that you're a mother or a single mother and that you have outside commitments. They want you for your job in a certain time frame and for you to put in so much. They don't care that you've had a bad day or that your daughter's sick and you need to get a baby-sitter or can't find a baby-sitter. They don't want to hear that."

At the office, these women epitomize calm and control. They remain focused under pressure. A glimpse into one successful executive's home life illustrates problems unseen by the outside world:

Margaret struggles with a sinking feeling every morning. Her sons are well liked at the local elementary school, yet it has become clear over a number of months that they are not being invited to participate in after-school activities. They tell her about missed parties, sleep overs, and movies the other children are attending. Margaret can't figure it out. Her kids are as nice as the other kids in the neighborhood. She sees their disappointment and desperately wants answers. Margaret decides to speak with the boys' guidance counselor, Mrs. Smith. She makes an appointment.

Mrs. Smith gets right to the point. She taps her pencil briskly. "Quite frankly, Margaret, at your children's ages, the driving force behind their relationships is your relationship with their friends' parents. You simply haven't developed a camaraderie with the other boys' parents. If you could take some time off during the day to work in the library or volunteer in the office, you'd meet a lot of the other mothers. I'm sure that would help to remedy this situation."

Margaret is dismayed. Mrs. Smith might just as well have told her to earn the Nobel Prize in medicine. Managing a $20 million budget, 1,500 employees in eight cities, and an office staff of twenty-five leaves little time for volunteering during the day. Margaret hardly has time to cross her legs, much less arrange books on a library shelf. She can't just excuse herself from a national sales meeting to "run out for a few hours to help out at the school."

Guilt and indecision. Margaret is plagued by them. Her professional responsibilities and her maternal demands are once again at odds. If she chooses to put her career first, her kids will suffer. If she's there for her kids the way she wants to be, she'll fall behind at the office and jeopardize her job. Margaret is miserable. There is no workable solution in sight that will please everyone.

Margaret is right. There *isn't* an immediate solution to her problem. The consensus among women in the FESS study is that you have to be able to split your personality—leaving such roles as mother and wife and household caretaker at home when you get in the car to go to work every morning, and reversing the process each evening.

"I've dealt with tremendous guilt for working and being away from my daughters," says another executive whose children are now grown. "I was always torn between being at work where it was interesting and being at home when I needed to be needed. No matter where you were, you were in the wrong place."

Many of these women feel enormous culpability about their dual roles. "I always felt guilty for having to go back to work," one says. "I always wanted to be that at-home mom and be there for my kids."

An executive who works fifty to sixty hours a week and travels at least half of that time says she deals with her household responsibilities by having a "high tolerance for dust." Still, she says, "there's really that lack of control of my own time that is a serious stress to me."

Having no time for themselves is a universal complaint among executive women. "Because of my schedule, my life is either my job or my family. We have no social life, so I would say that is a heavy stress," one executive says.

> The consensus among women in the FESS study is that you have to be able to split your personality—leaving such roles as mother and wife and household caretaker at home when you get in the car to go to work every morning, and reversing the process each evening.

"In a normal week," says another woman, "I probably work fifty to sixty hours. I do a lot of traveling, and it goes in fits and spurts. Some months I'll be traveling maybe 50 to 60 percent of the time, and then other months 20 percent. That lack of control of my own time is a serious stress item to me."

"All I do is work. I have no external relationships," is another common litany among today's female executives. The problem stems not from a lack of desire or opportunity, but from not having the time to take advantage of them. Says one executive, "I don't have a lot of time on my hands. In fact, I'm going through my invitations right now, and I really have to sort through them. I have to decline a lot of them because I just don't have the time."

Despite these difficulties, women continue to climb into the top ranks of corporations. A 1990 survey by *Fortune* magazine found that 40 percent of the nation's managers and administrators were women. Yet, of the 4,102 highest-paid executives listed for the 799 public companies on the Fortune 1000 list of industrial and service companies, only nineteen were women. Similarly, from a list of 9,293 division heads and assistant vice-presidents in 255 of the country's largest corporations, only 5 percent were women. A Korn/Ferry International study of the boards of this country's largest corporations demonstrates progress in this seemingly dismal situation: 60 percent of large corporations now have a female director as compared to 11 percent twenty years ago. And a 1992 study by Rebecca M. J. Yates, director of the master of business administration program at the University of Dayton in Ohio and Roy D. Adler, professor at Pepperdine University in California, indicates that, albeit in smaller numbers, women are climbing the corporate ladder faster than men are.

More than two hundred Fortune 500 companies responding to an Adler-Yates survey reported on the career histories of three hundred executive women. The study found that the percentage of women in the top twenty jobs had increased from a mere 1 percent in 1980 to 7.5 percent in 1992.

The study also found a correlation between women who received MBAs and those who would become top executives twenty years later. Historically, the researchers said, twenty-five years had been the minimum amount of experience needed to enter such positions. While in 1967 women represented only 2.6 percent of the MBA graduates, in 1992—twenty-five years later—women had claimed 7.5 percent of the top spots. Today, women make up 30 percent of the pool of MBA graduates. Based on their numbers, researchers Adler and Yates predict that up to 20 percent of the top corporate jobs will be held by women by the year 2000.

As these and other studies show, while not completely shattered, the glass ceiling has been raised for women, by women. Good news? Absolutely. But unless the corporate atmosphere changes drastically, more and more women will be subject to the stresses that could lead to Female Executive Stress Syndrome.

CHAPTER 3

What We Know
about Stress

THERE IS PLENTY of good news about females and stress. While early studies targeted men, during the last decade, studies about women, men, and stress have become more sensitive to gender differences. The first studies that involved women and looked at gender differences were hopelessly flawed. Since women in the workforce were often in support positions, and men were often in decision-making positions, studies explaining stress differences on the basis of gender alone were invalid. In other words, findings that said women suffered more stress could be explained equally as well by assuming that people in decision-making or executive positions (i.e., mostly men) suffered less from stress than did people in support positions (i.e., mostly women).

Recent studies show that there are many areas of work-related stress where there are no gender differences. That's the good news detailed later in this chapter. The bad news is that there are still many aspects of corporate America that place undue stress upon women. There are great gaps in the research on women and stress, leaving much to be done before we can offer solutions to stressed-out women in the workforce. Our intent with the FESS study is to help fill in some of these gaps.

Hundreds of studies have been conducted on stress and its various components. We cannot pretend to offer a comprehensive review of all of these studies. Instead, we will focus on studies conducted in the last ten years that examine gender differences and other dimensions of stress explored by the FESS study. Our intention is to provide a brief background of relevant stress research that will enable a more thorough understanding of the results of the FESS study.

What is stress?

STRESS HAS BEEN DEFINED as "any demand that creates tension, or threat and requires a change or adaptation" (Coleman, Morris, and Glaros, 1987). We all have felt stress, both good and bad. Getting married, buying your first car or house, having your first child, all are "good" stresses. Divorce, a death in the family, getting fired from your job, and other such events are the negative varieties of stress. We all experience stress every day: it is an intricate part of living that cannot be avoided. Stress, if used wisely, can be a tremendous facilitator of growth. When most people talk about experiencing stress, they actually are referring to *distress*, which involves the negative and potentially harmful forms of stress. "Stressors" refer to situations, events, or people in our lives that produce stressful physical, mental, or emotional responses. People vary tremendously in their reactions to stress; it is quite possible for two people to react in completely different ways to the same stressor.

Much of the research on stress focuses on selective coping strategies that aid individuals in effectively handling stressful situations. As you might expect, coping skills vary from person to person. Those who cope effectively might not experience the same damaging effects from stress suffered by those who do not.

Life situations affecting stress

SOME RECENT STUDIES indicate that a higher level of "perceived control" (i.e., a belief that one *does* control the outcome of a specific situation) might help individuals reduce their negative reactions to stress (Amatea and Fong, 1991; Tetrick and La Rocco, 1987). This suggests that perceived control builds self-confidence in one's abilities to cope effectively with problems. Another study, however, found no significant association between perceived control and stress reactions (Knight, 1990). One possible explanation is that the subjects in the Knight study might have been confronted with situations that they could *not* control; in that case, persistent efforts at taking control might produce repeated frustrations and failures. The following situation illustrates this point:

Chelsea has had enough. She is worn out, angry, and confused. Every job she has had in the past has been great. Her skills in finance and portfolio management are legend. At thirty-five she is shrewd, respected, and confident. Her secretary even teases her about her morning entrance. The double doors to the suite fly open, Chelsea runs through, a blur of color, as she heads for her daily stacks of papers, reports, and unopened mail. There is no mistake about it: Chelsea is a woman with a mission, geared for success. She seems to have a "direct line" to the executive suite.

That is, she did. Until now. Chelsea has hit a problem she can't solve. Her supervisor, Annette, had seemed fine at first. She had smiled sweetly that first day in the meeting when Chelsea had been promoted and reassigned to Annette's team. Offering her hand, she spoke directly about the new responsibilities facing Chelsea and pledged her help and guidance in any issues that arose. There was no hint of undermining or betrayal from Annette. She was all "sweetness and light" for the first six months, flawless in her demeanor. No, Chelsea thinks, Annette would never be that obvious in her tactics. She considers that behavior sloppy and unprofessional. Annette's a piranha, on you before you can stop her, dismantling years of work and effort, tearing apart your self-esteem.

Chelsea finally understands her boss. Annette will cut her throat with the best blade of all—destroying Chelsea's work in slow, methodical ways. Not everything will be wrong, of course; just enough to make a case for dismissal. There is no way for Chelsea to prove any of this. Business is business.

Chelsea feels a little like a sheep going to slaughter. She is sure there is nothing she can do to change the outcome. She has tried in vain to please Annette. And yet, repeatedly, Annette tells her in a silken voice, "I know, Chelsea, that you gave this project your best, but it's just not quite up to what I was looking for. Good luck on that rewrite, and don't close the door on your way out." At those moments, Chelsea wants to lunge across the desk and strangle this woman. Nothing she does, says, or even thinks makes a difference. This aspect of her life is out of her control and she is furious.

Chelsea's situation is a tough one. So how *can* a woman keep adverse business circumstances from ruling her life? A few studies focusing on women found evidence that career women who are married and have families appear to be both physically and emotionally healthier than career women who are single (Amatea and Fong, 1991; Fong and Amatea, 1992; Long, Kahn, & Schultz, 1992). One of these studies discovered that married working mothers who held so-called "traditional beliefs" did not feel as threatened by stressors at work. The researchers speculated that these women might not be as invested in their careers. As a result, they would be expected to place more value on noncareer aspects of life, rendering their jobs and any related stresses less important to them.

Several studies investigated the relationship between social and/or family support and work stress. The findings were inconsistent, with some studies producing evidence that positive work relationships helped reduce stress (Amatea and

Fong, 1991; King and Winett, 1986), while others failed to support this relationship (Tettrich and La Rocco, 1987). One study found that work-related stress decreased when married partners engaged in dual career planning and positive support of their spouse's career (Steffy and Ashbaugh, 1986). Related findings suggested that many professional women felt much of their stress was caused by the lack of personal time for themselves after work (King and Winett, 1986). However, another study produced findings suggesting that effective coping might have less to do with time available after work than with the ability to simply relax after work, regardless of the demands that exist outside work (Long, 1988).

Other studies examined the relationship between stress and the desire to pursue a career. These studies found that women who preferred having careers over staying home with children experienced less emotional distress when they returned to work soon after their child's birth. In contrast, women who were working to meet financial needs rather than from a wish for a career tended to experience more difficulties coping in these circumstances, both at work and at home (DeMeis, Hock, and McBride, 1986; King and Winett, 1986).

Personality factors reducing stress

ONE STUDY FOUND EVIDENCE to suggest that career women with a more "egalitarian attitude" (i.e., more feminist-like attitudes) experienced higher levels of stress in reaction to high-stress jobs that offered little emotional support from fellow workers (Long, Kahn, and Schultz, 1992). The researchers speculated that working women with less egalitarian beliefs might not have been as stressed by work environments that are still dominated by men and possibly discriminate against women.

A few studies attempted to identify specific personality traits or personality types that are resistant or immune to the negative effects of stress. One study investigated the previously researched personality trait of "hardiness" (i.e., being strong, durable, optimistic, and able to bounce back quickly), and its ability to insulate individuals from the negative effects of stress (Manning, Williams, and Wolfe, 1988). Although these researchers found some support for this concept, others did not, causing speculation that "hardiness" actually might result from, instead of cause, extended periods of good mental and physical health.

Another study examined a personality trait labeled "negative affectivity," which is described as a cynical, pessimistic, and perpetually distressed outlook (Parkes, 1990). This study discovered that "negative affectivity" made individuals more vulnerable or more overreactive to stress at work, since they appeared to believe that the dire consequences they constantly anticipated had arrived whenever new demands or expectations were placed upon them at work.

An abundance of research has searched for specific coping strategies or personal resources that are found in more successful and effective individuals. Some studies have found evidence to support the assumption that coping strategies emphasizing planning and active behavior in problem solving appear to reduce stress successfully (Long, 1988; Long, Kahn, and Schultz, 1992; Parkes, 1990). One of these studies also found evidence suggesting that a defensive strategy called "suppression" (described as adaptive strategies of "restraint," "compromise," and "continuing with immediate activities regardless of difficulties") seems to be strongly related to low levels of distress (Parkes, 1990). This study concluded that suppression is most adaptive in a situation where the individual has little or no control; she is able to stop hitting her head against a brick wall and successfully pursue other activities without experiencing high levels of distress. This latter study emphasized the value of tenacity and self-reliance, since these characteristics appeared to insulate many individuals from experiencing stress in reaction to high work demands and/or little or no support from co-workers.

Stress similarities between men and women

STUDIES COMPARING GROUPS of men against groups of women with respect to various components of stress have discovered many similarities. A few such studies have discovered that men and women experience significant disruption in both their level of job satisfaction and the quality of marital and family relationships in reaction to highly demanding and monopolizing careers (Bedeian, Burke, and Moffett, 1988; Nelson, Quick, and Hitt, 1989). These researchers concluded that excessive demands of energy and time from high-stress careers had the ability to compromise the quality of family relationships and general career satisfaction. One study examining level of job commitment found no significant differences between men and women (Chusmir, 1986), while a related study found no significant differences between men and women in stress produced by their levels of satisfaction with "career progress" (Nelson, Quick, and Hitt, 1989). Researchers examining hundreds of companies for their levels of success and the frequency of going out of business concluded that there were no differences between businesses headed by women and those headed by men (Kallenberg and Leicht, 1991). Other studies found no significant gender differences in how individuals reacted to specific stressful characteristics of the job environment (Crabbs, Black, and Morton, 1986; DiSalvo, Lubbers, Rossi, and Lewis, 1988).

Several studies have examined gender differences in specific coping strategies for dealing with stress. McDonald and Korabik (1991) found no significant differences between the use of action-oriented, "problem-focused" coping strategies by male and female managers. This study also found that there was no gender difference in the tendency to increase the use of "wishful thinking" as a coping strategy in reaction to high levels of stress. In addition, there were no gender differences in the reported overall levels of general job stress. A related study discovered that both male and female senior administrators believed that their talents, abilities, and willingness to work hard were vital to their own career successes. However, when they were asked to describe general formulas for career success, both groups believed these same characteristics were more important to the success formulas of women than men (Russo, Kelly, and Deacon, 1991). These results also suggested that both sexes might view relationships with professional colleagues and associates as more vital to the formulas for career success of men than of women. Thus, the viewpoint seemed to be that women make it on ability and men make it on sociability.

Several research studies discovered significant differences in their comparisons of men and women with regard to stress. A few studies concluded that married women experienced more internal stress and more relationship conflicts than their married male counterparts, seemingly due to a higher level of conflict or incompatibility between career and home/family roles (Bedeian, Burke, and Moffett, 1988; McDonald and Korabik, 1991). One of the studies added to these findings by citing evidence that only career women appeared to be bothered significantly by dissatisfaction with child-care arrangements at home. This supported the idea that men tend to leave their family roles and responsibilities at home when they go to work, while women seem to take these worries to work with them and think about them during work hours. Another study discovered that bosses were more likely to promote and to give raises to women who emphasized their family roles over their careers; at the same time, they were more likely to promote and give raises to men who stressed their careers over their families. Men and women who showed opposite patterns were not rewarded nearly as well by their superiors (Lobel and St. Clair, 1992).

Corporate America is replete with working mothers who face myriad problems as they juggle the responsibilities of their two worlds. Following is the story of one such woman:

Kendall stares out the rain-splattered window of her high-rise office, the gloomy gray light reflecting her mood. She has worked through another lunch, desperately trying to make up for lost time. Michael, her two-year-old, is sick for the fourth time this year, his allergies causing repeated sore throats and earaches. She thinks about the long night she spent, pacing with her small son in her arms as she tried to comfort him. Alone again because Jeff was in Europe on business.

Kendall wonders how he always manages to be away when things hit the fan. On the other hand, Jeff's cheerful, easygoing attitude makes Kendall think she is losing it. She told her best friend, Melanie, "I think I'm going crazy. Here Jeff is a corporate attorney with his own problems at work, but he's always great with Michael. Nothing gets to him. I crack up when he spills his milk!"

Kendall knows her job performance has fallen in the past few weeks. Her career is vital to her, and she tries to concentrate on the work in front of her. The first year after Michael's birth had been fine. She had hired a nanny to look after him. Margarita was congenial, hardworking, and great with Michael. But when Margarita left for six weeks, Kendall began to fall apart. What in the world is she supposed to do now? A single tear slaps the papers in front of her.

Kendall knows she has to move quickly or she will fall further behind at work, but she also feels disoriented. Whenever things are out of place with Michael,

F E S S

Kendall just can't concentrate. Her lack of sleep clouds her mind like a fog; she becomes illogical.

She shakes her head vigorously. She will find a solution. There is no way she will allow another week to go like this one. Kendall is going to take back control. Her first job is to find a new nanny.

By logically analyzing her problem, Kendall is able to come to a solution. It is this kind of focus that helps many women succeed in business. There are other characteristics that mark executive women as well. Two studies examining the presence of Machiavellian tendencies (exploitative and manipulative) discovered that women were far more likely to display Machiavellian tendencies than their male peers (Burnett, Hunt, and Chonko, 1986; Gable and Topol, 1988). Although this might appear to suggest that women may need to be Machiavellian to succeed in the American patriarchy, one of the studies discovered the level of Machiavellianism in women actually decreased as seniority, executive levels of power, and income increased. As women rose in power and prestige, they no longer had to engage in trench warfare.

Some studies investigated the relationship between gender and experiencing "sex-role conflict." Women scored significantly higher than men in "sex-role conflict," indicating that women do experience far higher levels of

> Women were far more likely to display Machiavellian tendencies than their male peers...Although this might appear to suggest that women may need to be Machiavellian to succeed in the American patriarchy, the level of Machiavellianism in women actually decreased as seniority, executive levels of power, and income increased.

stress in reaction to conflicts between career and roles as wife and mother (Chusmir, 1986; Greenglass, Pantony, and Burke, 1988). Women feel torn between two worlds. One study indicated that women experience more stress in a wider variety of work situations than do men (Crabbs, Black, and Morton, 1986). However, another study discovered that men experienced more stress when they had problems or conflicts in work relationships, while women experienced more stress when job responsibilities were increased and when they were required to exercise power (DiSalvo, Lubbers, Rossi, and Lewis, 1988). Although the latter finding seems to imply that women have more conflicts over exercising power than men do, this could be due to subordinates who have trouble obeying a female supervisor at work. This finding was replicated in a study that also discovered a significant stress level among women in reaction to sexual discrimination on the job (McDonald and Korabik, 1991).

Another study examining the meaningfulness of work for men and women concluded that meaningful work is more important to women, since they appear to be more likely to leave jobs not seen as meaningful (Miller and Wheeler, 1992). Women want their work to make a difference in the world. There was evidence from this study that women might not experience obvious sexual discrimination in lower-level promotions relatively early in their careers, but might experience more sexual discrimination in later promotions leading to executive leadership positions. The closer they got to the glass ceiling, the higher it was raised. A related study found that female professionals experienced significantly more stress than their male peers from "organizational politics" (Nelson, Quick, and Hitt, 1989). These researchers concluded that women might be at a disadvantage in their efforts to play office politics because the rules of office politics are dictated by men and favor men. Evidence also suggested that the men in the sample might have been less likely to admit to their emotional distress than the women in the sample. Men were more likely than women to control their levels of reported emotional distress through physical exercise and sporting activities.

Gender differences in coping strategies

A FEW STUDIES found evidence indicating that men attempt to cope with stress by seeking emotional support among fellow workers and tend to engage in distracting activities outside of work, such as hobbies or sports, while women attempt to cope with stress by seeking family sources of social support and by talking about their feelings about work problems to others (Bedeian, Burke, and Moffett, 1988; McDonald and Korabik, 1991). It was suggested that, although career women might be subjected to a wider variety of stressors than career men, they appear to cope better with stresses on the job. A study investigating the coping strategies of male and female teachers under high levels of stress found that the male teachers were far more likely to utilize a coping strategy the researchers labeled "depersonalization," involving an emotional withdrawal of interest in and concern for their students (Ogus, Greenglass, and Burke, 1990). This study suggested that women coped better with work-related stress because they were more energetic and because they valued and relied upon their emotional friendships, as in the following example:

Maryanne walks briskly toward the cafeteria. She hopes to find her friend, Jane, before the 8:30 meeting Mr. Johnston, the district manager, has called for all supervisors. Attendance is mandatory, so Maryanne knows he means business. Sales have fallen for their division this quarter; heads will roll.

They'll go through the usual song and dance. These boys "up top" don't get the message. Retail sales are depressed nationally. Maryanne and her people **have** done their jobs. They are not responsible for national trends. Maryanne wants to crawl under a rock somewhere. She feels her blood pressure rising.

Jane is in another division, immune from the rise and fall of corporate sales. She is always calming, but direct, when Maryanne hits a roadblock. Maryanne doesn't want the truth sugarcoated. If that's the kind of support she needed she'd call her mother. She's a capable adult and she needs another perspective—an honest one. Jane has an uncanny talent for striking a balance between identifying painful realities and maintaining hope. She's an invaluable and loyal friend who has seen Maryanne through a hundred corporate crises. Maryanne needs help through one more.

Jane's shoulder-length, chestnut brown hair glistens in the morning sun. She greets Maryanne with a smile. "I'd know those footsteps anywhere!" Maryanne looks around the cafeteria for a private setting. She's the team leader and wants privacy. She doesn't want her staff to see how worried she is. While Maryanne glances furtively around the room, Jane intuitively assesses that Maryanne is extremely uneasy. Quickly she says, "Maryanne, you look really worried. It's 7:45, and you've got forty-five minutes to get your head straight. Let's go to my office so you can vent in peace." Maryanne smiles, nods in agreement, and dutifully follows Jane down the hall. Jane will be a great sounding board. She always has been. Talks like these make all the difference. Jane is a light in a very dark night.

Gender differences and burnout

IN RECENT YEARS, burnout has garnered attraction from many researchers. Initially, burnout referred specifically to people who worked in careers involving high interpersonal contact with clients. But in more recent years, this concept has been broadened to include all types of careers. Definitions of burnout differ in their complexity and the variety of components involved. One general definition of burnout was cited by Dolan and Renaud (1992) as "the syndrome of physical and emotional exhaustion involving the development of negative self-concept, negative job attitudes, and loss of feeling and concern for clients." Many research studies have debated whether burnout is related primarily to environmental factors or to personality variables. After reviewing several research studies addressing burnout, Dolan and Renaud (1992) concluded that burnout is a complex interaction of individual needs and resources with the various demands and frustrations found in the work environment.

One study exploring burnout in a large sample of male and female teachers discovered that burnout was related to work environments characterized by high production demands and high levels of conflict (Burke and Greenglass, 1989). Another study examining male and female senior executives concluded that the high levels of responsibility seemed to be the chief variable in promoting burnout, although personality variables such as low self-esteem and a self-centeredness or self-orientation were important, as well (Dolan and Renaud, 1992). This study also found that individuals who were willing to take risks in their high-stress jobs experienced a high sense of personal accomplishment.

Some stress can be *positive*. But internalized and in large doses, it can be devastating. Stress must be properly channeled. Women heavily invested in their careers might be putting themselves at risk for burnout. Take the case of Brenda:

Brenda can't keep this up. She has loved her work for the past fifteen years and has devoted herself to advancing faster than anyone else. She is sure she has made the correct career decisions at critical times. She's a survivor. Brenda prides herself on being a perceptive judge of people. She has avoided disaster countless times by relying on her "gut." Her instincts have never failed her—until last year.

The depression in the computer business shocked no one. Industry forecasts predicted a downturn in computer stock for weeks. Her company, a midsized, Midwest-based organization, had weathered many storms in its ten-year history, so this was nothing new. That's what they thought.

Until last year, Brenda had heard the word "downsizing" only in trade magazines. Now she has a front-row seat for the downsizing drama that is affecting her company like a cancer. For many women and men, dreams of full and prosperous careers are being replaced with stark severance packages. Financial survival stalks the decision makers and stifles creativity. No longer do her people feel like the best and the brightest. Brenda needs to transfuse herself and her staff with hope and energy.

In talking with her psychologist that afternoon, Brenda realizes how responsible she has always felt for people who work for her. She rolls her eyes and sighs. "I know I'm an eternal caretaker. My stomach knots up when I have to announce another layoff. It's almost as if I'm losing my job. I'm getting burned out and think about running away to Hawaii every day."

Brenda realizes that there are limits to what she can do. She can't act as a lifeguard for every employee. She knows that if she doesn't stop feeling so responsible for corporate decisions that she didn't make in the first place, she'll burn out completely and be no good for anyone—including herself. If she's to survive, she has to establish firm limits for herself, keeping her job in perspective and not investing so heavily in it. After all, her primary responsibility is to herself, and that is the key to her future and the basis for her business success.

Brenda's caretaking is perhaps a part of her femininity that she must learn to control if she is to protect herself in the business world. In a study investigating the relationships between burnout and "social role orientation" as measured by the Bem Sex-Role Inventory (Eichinger, Heifetz, and Ingraham, 1991), researchers redefined the Bem Sex-Role Inventory "masculine" score as indicating "instrumentality," (i.e., a logical, fix-it approach to problems) and the Bem Sex-Role Inventory "feminine" score as indicating "expressivity" (i.e., an emotional, let-it-all-out style). They concluded that a "balanced social role orientation" associated with the combination of high levels of instrumentality and expressivity was associated with higher levels of job satisfaction and lower levels of job stress.

Another study investigating the relationship between burnout and "hardiness" (Holt, Fine, and Tollefson, 1987) found that a group of teachers in high-stress environments who displayed low levels of burnout appeared to possess several of the characteristics of "hardiness," while the group of teachers in high-stress environments who displayed high burnout did not possess these characteristics. It was concluded that "hardiness" increased the capacity to cope with stress successfully.

Gender differences in burnout were investigated in a large sample of managers and nonmanagers. Stressful emotionally oriented work relationships appeared to be a primary source of burnout in women, while stressful work relationships of a more personal, competitive, and goal-oriented basis were a primary source of burnout in men (Pretty, McCarthy, and Catano, 1992).

An excellent review of the research studies addressing gender differences in burnout was conducted by Greenglass (1991). This review scrutinized the widespread assumption that women experienced more burnout than men. Greenglass found that the research contradicted this assumption. Instead, research shows that outside careers were not more harmful to the health of mothers than they were to women without children, and that women who were employed outside the home actually appeared to enjoy better physical health than did homemakers. Greenglass concluded that multiple life roles did not necessarily produce higher levels of stress or more physical illness in women. Other research evidence cited by Greenglass indicated that women actually seemed to experience less burnout than their male peers. Men's burnout was produced chiefly by work-related stress, while women's burnout was produced by a wide variety of factors, which included work stress, conflict between career versus wife-and-mother roles, problems with social relationships, and marital conflicts. Greenglass also cited research addressing coping with burnout that indicated "instrumental coping" works equally well for men and women in dealing with career anxiety. Some studies investigating the relationship between burnout and "Type A" behavior patterns linked to coronary artery heart problems found that "women, compared to the men, were not only more hard-driving, competitive, and achievement-oriented as defined by the Type A behavior pattern, but they also tended to use more problem-focused coping than men when confronted with job anxiety" (Greenglass, 1991).

F
E
S
S

Understanding stress

IN SUMMARY, life situations that appear to reduce stress include higher levels of perceived control (probably correlated with higher job rank and more power), stable marital and family situations, and a woman's earnest desire to pursue a career.

Life situations that appear to reduce stress include higher levels of perceived control...stable marital and family situations, and a woman's earnest desire to pursue a career.

Some studies support the value of positive work and/or social relationships in reducing stress, but other studies do not. Women with more feminist-equality attitudes experience more stress in the patriarchal workplace, while women who are able to maintain a positive, self-confident, and optimistic attitude experience less stress. Coping strategies thought to reduce stress include deliberate and methodical problem-solving behaviors, as well as the flexibility to stop trying to improve situations where little or no control exists and to carry on with more effective actions in other areas. It's important to know when to give up and move on to better things.

Allowing overly demanding careers to monopolize one's life seems to increase stress for both men and women. Career women are more prone to experience stress at work from situations outside work, such as unacceptable child-care

F
E
S
S

arrangements or conflicts in social relationships, while men seem to experience stress at work almost entirely from problems and conflicts in the workplace itself.

A high number of junior career women who have not reached executive levels of power display extreme Machiavellian tendencies. While many career women experience stress when they exercise the power of their positions, it is unclear whether this is caused by internal conflicts about wielding power or by external conflicts with subordinates who do not readily accept directions from a woman.

Women seem to require that their work be meaningful and important. Unfortunately, they remain at a stressful disadvantage in their efforts to play office politics, which continue to occur almost exclusively on male turf. Working women cope with stress by seeking support in relationships outside work and talking openly about their feelings toward their jobs, while working men prefer to cope with stress by seeking support from fellow workers and engaging in distracting, non-work-related activities.

Some studies suggest that women are better able to cope with stress than men are. One study actually found that a "balanced" orientation, combining both "masculine" and "feminine" characteristics, was the most effective approach for successfully coping with stress. Contrary to prior assumptions, studies suggest that women are *less* susceptible to career burnout than men, and career women with families experience less stress and fewer physical health problems than stay-at-home mothers.

CHAPTER 4

How Is Female Executive Stress Syndrome Different?

OR YEARS she had sailed along over every hurdle, graduating at the top of her class, being the "first" woman to achieve each rung of the corporate ladder on her way up, until one day, she hit a roadblock—either in her career or her personal relationships. What should have been a small blow to her self-esteem was the proverbial last straw that landed her in my office.

Since 1985, woman after woman has walked into my office suffering similar symptoms. Sometimes they were undermined by another woman at work, or they had been discriminated against in some way. Other times they had been passed over for a promotion or had been "promoted" into a hollow position that had more fluff than substance. Generally, they were having some type of difficulty in their central love relationship or had come to the end of a long-term relationship or marriage. Often they had outgrown their husbands, who still found them attractive, and were having not-so-secret affairs.

Most of them were referred by their doctors, usually their gynecologists, after they had gone in for their annual exams and burst into tears. Over the next two to three years, into the late eighties, this trend became more obvious, and executive women became my primary clientele. I began to realize that each of my clients had sacrificed herself to professional success. As a result, she had not nurtured herself, and she had not nurtured relationships with the other people in her life. Due to her own neglect, she had virtually no support system.

During this time, as I began to formulate the characteristics of FESS and the solutions to this growing problem, I was having my second child. The larger I grew, the harder it was for me to present a purely professional image at the office. Unexpectedly, my pregnancy, my ability to successfully integrate my love of having babies into my professional career, became a part of therapy. Before I'm misquoted as saying every executive should get pregnant to solve her problems, let me be crystal clear—there are many ways of expressing a feminine side having nothing to do with having children or even being married. My being obviously pregnant during this time, however, helped me and my clients focus on the integration of femininity and the professional arena where it has largely been shunned. Believe me, they couldn't miss it. Today, I keep pictures of my children prominently displayed in my office to serve the same purpose. I want my clients to know they don't have to sacrifice their femininity to ensure their success.

Many of these women had ignored their feminine side and their personal lives for decades. To gain power in the workplace, they had separated from and essentially forgotten their personal feminine side and aligned themselves with all of the adjectives typically associated with successful men—driven, cutthroat, single minded, unshakable. Now, as they found themselves teetering on the edge of a breakdown—perhaps even slipping over the edge—they realized that they had to reintegrate these forgotten sides if they wanted to become whole. They had to do this to survive.

> To gain power in the workplace, they had separated from and essentially forgotten their personal feminine side and aligned themselves with all of the adjectives typically associated with successful men—driven, cutthroat, single-minded, unshakable.

FESS as a hybrid

THE WOMAN WITH FESS suffers from a hybrid form of stress. Her problems are neither like that of the nonworking woman or the male executive. And while the breakdown itself may be similar to other breakdowns that turn a functioning person into a debilitated one, her recovery is unique.

While male executive stress may be earmarked by the same driven behavior present in FESS, males have far more support both in the workplace and at home upon which they can draw for sustenance and recovery. Men usually have a ready outlet— golf on Sunday, season tickets with a buddy to professional sporting events, tennis on Thursday nights—to help release the tension that can build from being on the hot seat at work month after month. In addition, the majority of executive men still have stay-at-home wives who handle much of the stress of running a household for them, while the executive woman, though she may not be scrubbing the toilets herself, is still responsible for making sure the job gets done. If there's not food in the refrigerator, it's her fault. If the child is sick, she has to get him to the doctor.

Similarly, the executive woman's stress is far different from the stresses of women who stay at home. Women who do not earn an income have the backing of our patriarchal society. They do not threaten a man's power because their role does not overlap his role. Housewives face different challenges of organization, prioritization, and learning to balance their needs against the needs of family members. It is a tough job and should be viewed with pride. Their challenges, however, are different from those faced by the executive woman because they operate within a family circle, not a business.

On any given day, the executive women may have 150 personalities at work to appease. She has a budget to balance and statistics to review. If she blows the business deal, there is no second chance. Her world is a bottom-line, "cut to the chase" test every day she is there. She either produces or she does not. If she fails to perform, she's out of a job.

The executive lives in a complex and constantly shifting world where she is always on stage in front of a critical audience. On the other hand, housewives have more opportunities to socialize and build support networks. The executive woman usually has no ready support system. She simply doesn't have time. Friendships are nurtured "on the run." The executive is therefore denied access to this coping mechanism used by healthy women, i.e., sharing feelings with other women. With few friends to turn to when times are bad, executive women usually internalize whatever they are feeling. Their isolation adds to their stress. Taking the time to build friendships can be time well spent, paying big dividends in periods of personal or professional crisis. Without close relationships, as Rebecca finds out, coping with life stresses becomes more difficult:

Rebecca wonders how in the world she will ever finish. The floor of the advertising firm is quiet, dark, abandoned. The clock on her desk reminds her of another broken promise to leave work by seven like other "normal" girlfriends. Jack's muttered acknowledgment when she'd called to tell him she'd be late again betrayed his obvious disgust. He'd hung up without saying goodbye, having given up pleasantries and cordiality months ago.

Jack never understood the urgency that marked her world. "To stand in my shoes would be difficult because I'm always on the run," she'd told him. She had been this way for years, and her hard work had paid off. The number one producer in her firm last year, she had been awarded the local advertising community's award for "brightest new star" at the banquet. Mr. Thompson, the firm's CEO, positioned himself next to her that evening. He was showing his approval and endorsing her future. She knew she had earned every minute of it.

Rebecca is convinced that she is right in living this way—for now. Career first, marriage and kids later. It makes sense to postpone marriage to Jack until she's offered a partnership in the firm. It certainly wouldn't be fair to plan a wedding between flights. And they've lived together for five years, so it's not like any of this is a surprise to him. In fact, when Rebecca was hired by the firm, he was as thrilled as she was. This is her shot. She knows that. But now she's afraid the rules are changing, and she desperately wants Jack to stay a part of her life.

Up on the forty-fourth floor, Rebecca cannot avoid the painful truth. Jack has withdrawn from her. Rebecca feels isolated. Without Jack, a lot of her life just doesn't make sense. If he leaves her, she's convinced she'll be alone forever. Jack is irreplaceable. Where will she find another man with his sense of humor, his education, his social savvy? A guy who's willing to put up with her ambition and drive?

Rebecca forbids herself to start thinking about the wreckage of previous relationships, but it happens any-way—the rejection when boyfriends couldn't handle her higher salary or professional success. She grew weary from the revolving door of men, all of whom suffered from inflated egos. For a woman to outearn them, they were stripped of their masculinity. Please!

Rebecca picks up the phone, then puts it back down. She has nobody to call. She wants to talk to Ann, her roommate from Penn, but it's been two years since they've seen each other. Charlotte, her high school girl-friend, is in Seattle on business. Natalie, her pal from the health club, is married with a kid. Probably home in bed with her husband like most women, Rebecca thinks. She doesn't want to call out of the blue, in the middle of the night, in a growing state of panic. Jack is really her only contact, and he sure isn't talking to her.

Work has prevented her from being with other women, from having those conversations only another woman can understand. She remembers those late-night chats in dark college bars that made her feel so understood and included. Now, in addition to the "Jack ache," Rebecca misses her buddies. She needs female conversation. She recalls the nights of stargazing on the dorm roof. With their Diet Cokes in hand, they solved the problems of the world and became "one with the universe." The world made so much sense then. They were women, and they were loyal to each other, to their femininity, and to their futures. There is no other feeling of belonging that compares.

Rebecca is almost crying. Where are her girl-friends now? She has to admit that she hasn't kept the friendships going. She has put her career and Jack ahead of everyone and everything else. I guess I deserve what I'm getting, she thinks. It's time to reach out. This time, she'll take care of her friendships—she doesn't want to end up in this "blind alley" again. Rebecca picks up the phone.

As this situation demonstrates, women pay a price for career success. On the positive side, the executive provides her own financial security. And such security goes a long way. Countless marriages of women who do not work outside the home are based on the principle "He who earns the gold has the power." I have seen many of these women furious over this arrangement. As Sandra, a slender forty-two-year-old mother of four once told me: "I've made it possible for my husband to be successful by all the long hours I've worked at home, with the kids. He forgets my work when it comes to financial decisions. His needs come first and then I get the leftovers. I'd like to see him hire someone to work my hours—he'd pay a fortune!"

In most marriages between executives, the financial decisions are joint. A woman who earns a salary equal to her husband's expects to be taken seriously in decision making. Happily, executive women usually are great negotiators and have learned to work well with men. These skills can be invaluable in a marriage. Additionally, because she is financially independent, an executive woman can stay in a marriage out of choice, not economic necessity.

A lack of support both at work and away from work intensifies the stress faced by executive women. This is why FESS is truly a hybrid form of stress that is characterized by an internal dichotomy. This dichotomy, or duality, often is expressed by recovering patients who say they have had to learn to "think like a man and feel like a woman" to succeed and be healthy. Once they are able to recognize and validate their own feelings, they say they find a new power, a business savvy, political acumen, and clear thinking that enable them to progress geometrically both at work and in their personal lives.

Far too often, women who suffer from FESS align themselves entirely with the male way of thinking and acting and
cut themselves off completely from feeling. If they allow
themselves to feel at all, they compartmentalize their feelings,
only allowing themselves to feel small amounts a little bit at a
time. Like the character played by Holly Hunter in the movie
Broadcast News they take the phone off the hook and cry for
five minutes every morning, then dry their eyes and take on
the day.

Adding to their stress is their viewpoint:
they never see themselves as victims. They
are perfectionists who are used to taking
charge and accepting responsibility. If something goes wrong, they blame themselves,
even if this is a distortion of reality. They are
performers who are used to stuffing their feelings while they
achieve higher and higher goals. If they have a crying spell at
work, it devastates them, because they pride themselves on
being ice queens, immune to such mortal shortcomings. A
tearful episode doesn't fit in with managing multimillion dol-
lar budgets. By the time they get to my office, they are tor-
mented by all of the suffering they have shoved deep inside for
so many years.

> **A key characteristic of the FESS executive is the tremendous difficulty she has in asking for help.**

A key characteristic of the FESS executive is the tremendous difficulty she has in asking for help. These are endowed,
powerful women who are veterans at managing difficult
problems and resolving impossible dilemmas. Consulting a
psychologist may be the hardest thing they've ever forced
themselves to do. They feel deflated, defeated, exposed. As

one bright FESS woman said when she first sat down in my office, "I know I should have seen a psychologist years ago. I always thought I could use my job skills to solve my personal problems. It made sense, but it never seemed to work."

Being unable to apply job skill proficiency to their personal lives can be tremendously frustrating for FESS executives. On the surface, why shouldn't it work? Personal issues resemble the logical issues wrestled with at work. The FESS executive has to gradually understand that affairs of the heart require a different skill—an ability to use feelings and reflections, and, most importantly, one's intuitive self in resolving the problem at hand. Corporate America does not reward the latter approach, and career women have reacted to this by detaching from their feelings to survive and achieve in the patriarchy. These women often pay for this adaptation by losing touch with their own emotions and becoming maladaptive in their personal lives. The following case study illustrates what happens when one female executive refuses to acknowledge her feelings where work is concerned:

> Hope can't abide the idea of another trip out of town. An investment banker, she is already on a first-name basis with the stewardess on the red-eye shuttle to Chicago. Of course, no one can miss Hope—she's the woman with the laptop working at 3:00 A.M., drinking Perrier.
>
> Still single at forty-five, Hope is a striking slender blonde whose Swedish heritage shows in her fair complexion and delicate carriage. She had arrived in

New York twenty years earlier, "loaded for bear." She paid her dues in law school and was sent out to conquer the world of finance—which she did successfully. Precise, intense, and logical, Hope is a fierce adversary. She is always prepared, to the point, and three steps ahead of the men in the room. She had decided years ago to win—and win big. She refused to let a man out-deal her.

It is already midnight and Hope has only an hour to finish packing and get to the airport. Her cab is due soon; she will pick up her ticket at the gate.

She stares at her room. When was the last time she'd spent more than one night here? Her bed looks appealing, but forbidden. She reminds herself of her goal: to do the best for her client, even if she takes a hit in the process. She can't possibly refuse another trip just because she's tired. She has no time for fatigue.

Suddenly, she panics. Her hands are shaky and cold and breathing is difficult. The familiar dizziness and nausea grip her and the room fills with the sound of her heartbeat. Her psychologist had predicted this would happen. "Hope," Dr. Rainard had said, "if you don't start paying attention to yourself and your feelings, these panic attacks will increase."

So where was Dr. Rainard now? Boy, to go through another panic attack was the last thing she wanted. If only she could slow down, maybe these attacks would stop.

When does stress become a syndrome?

FEMALE EXECUTIVE STRESS SYNDROME (FESS) is a commonly occurring set of symptoms in reaction to a highly specific stressful situation. A syndrome is a constellation of behaviors (the FESS behaviors will be explained in greater detail in chapter 5) that appear again and again together. When these behaviors begin to interfere with your progress and success in life, when they become enduring and chronic as opposed to fleeting, it's time to get help.

The following charts can help you judge your FESS level. If you find yourself saying "yes" to many of these questions, you may suffer from FESS.

FESS symptoms
Are you a self-saboteur?

1. Is it difficult for you to say "no" or to draw lines?
2. Do you drink or smoke too much?
3. Do you hide your drinking or smoking?
4. Do you spend money to make yourself feel better?
5. Do you become worried when things begin to go well?
6. Are you unable to accept compliments with grace?
7. Do you belittle yourself when others compliment your achievements?
8. Do you feel undeserving of your position in life?
9. Have you chosen not to seek help when you realize there *is* a solution to your problems?

F
E
S
S

10. Do you become anxious when your relationships become rewarding? Do you anticipate disaster?

11. Do you choose to terminate relationships but regret your decision at a later time?

12. Do others describe you as emotionally reactive, antagonistic, or pessimistic?

13. If others become disappointed with you, do you become depressed?

14. Is there a little voice that repeatedly denies your success and achievements in life? Do you believe your little voice?

15. Does anticipation of failure prevent you from moving forward? Are you moving sideways?

16. Do you use your professional position as an excuse to avoid spending time with your spouse, friends, or children?

17. Are you a workaholic? Do you miss your work when you're vacationing?

18. Are you preoccupied with eating or dieting?

19. Do you feel guilty if you are not doing something you consider to be productive, profitable, or necessary?

20. Are you in an unhealthy relationship but don't know how to get out? Do you make excuses for staying in unhealthy relationships?

21. Has your circle of friends diminished significantly for no apparent reason?

22. Do you feel isolated?

23. Have you begun to have affairs because you don't have the time or energy for true relationships?

24. Do you have trouble sleeping or sleep too much?
25. Do you cry unexpectedly or have trouble crying in situations where crying would be expected?
26. Do you become irritable in situations you used to be able to handle smoothly?
27. Are you having panic attacks?
28. Do you have a strong desire to stop hurting or even brief thoughts of suicide to stop the hurting?
29. Have you begun to overreact to negative or even mediocre feedback at work?
30. When in desperation, do you retreat into seclusion instead of reaching out for help?

Rapid-fire therapy

ANOTHER DISTINGUISHING CHARACTERISTIC of women with FESS is their ability to progress rapidly through the therapy process. No years of psychoanalysis for them—they want results, ASAP, and they are willing to work hard for them.

Typically, therapy results in a slower-paced progress earned through weekly sessions with a therapist. The sessions are weekly so that more time can be devoted to therapy itself and underlying issues rather than catching up on a patient's current events. However, with executive women, I quickly adjusted therapy to fit their specific needs. I began to add Saturdays and nights to my practice. And frequent trips to Hong Kong, London, or Singapore on business meant weekly sessions with these very busy executives were not always possible. I found that even if we missed two weeks and then scheduled a session, these women cut through the chitchat with a sharpness I had not seen before.

It was apparent that during the time between sessions, they had been hard at work. They were constantly reflecting on what the last session had suggested to them. If a pattern between behavior and feelings had been explored, they came in with multiple examples of where this had occurred. A session that merely touched upon their relationship with their mother, for instance, would result in two to three sessions of memories and observations. They remembered the session themes, their feelings, and what I said to them each time.

Their swift intelligence dictated an accelerated form of therapy where points did not have to be reviewed repeatedly. They simply got it and moved on. As a result, the therapy was much more compact. When they set goals, they were focused on succeeding. Every time they left my office, they wanted a suggested reading list to reinforce what we had discussed that day and to help them prepare for our next session. If they had found their own book or article, they brought a copy for me or told me where to get it and at what price. They expected my full participation in all aspects of their progress. Each step of the way they wanted to know every "why" and "how."

These women also demanded a precision from me that I had never experienced before with patients. If I didn't use just the right term or word to describe a situation, they didn't let it pass unnoticed. If I described their situation incorrectly or missed their point, I heard about it.

Typically in therapy, a therapist says very little to allow the patients to activate themselves, come up with their own

F
E
S
S

answers, sort through the problems independently, and move on. The therapist doesn't want to lead a patient for fear they will become too dependent upon her for all of the answers. Instead, the therapist wants to foster autonomy and self-reliance.

With executive women, however, I found this traditional structure didn't work. They wanted to hear observations, and I had to tell them what I thought or they would be insulted. If I soft-pedaled my opinions, they would detect it immediately and then ask what I really thought and to please be blunt. There was little danger of them being led by the nose—they were on a mission, and I was a tool they used to help them reach a goal. Being in upper management, they knew all about intonation and body language and could read me—they couldn't be fooled even if I chose not to lend my observations. As a result, the therapy sessions for these women usually included my comments to help them bridge any gaps. They had an initial lack of emotional awareness, and I provided that for them until they were able to find their own feelings.

Their defenses were so well developed that, in the early stages of therapy, many of them could not even list common feelings for me and would ask that I provide a "list" of feelings for them. They were amazed at the range of feelings that existed, since so many of them either felt "okay" or "terrible" and had no experience with the spectrum of feeling most people experience. As one FESS woman commented, "Good soldiers don't feel, they just keep on marching."

Initial sessions with FESS patients were typically very emotional. Again, the dichotomy they lived every day was apparent in their inner-office versus outer-office behavior. In the waiting room, they were all business—perfection and precision in a $600 suit. Many of them brought briefcases, electronic Rolodexes, and cellular phones, just in case they needed a portable office while waiting in the reception area. Behind closed doors, however, their first sessions were very tearful as the pain flowed out of them. When the session was over, they buttoned up and walked out, staunch and unruffled. It was show time.

> When the session was over, they buttoned up and walked out, staunch and unruffled. It was show time.

FESS victims have a difficult time admitting the need for professional counseling. As the following example points out, however, strong women who occasionally take that helping hand actually are helping themselves:

Janice can't believe it has come to this. She runs a multimillion-dollar division, so why can't she get over a simple breakup with her boyfriend by herself? Calling a therapist is the last thing she wants to do.

Her girlfriend, Marsha, recommended Dr. Blanchard six months ago. At first, Janice was offended by Marsha's suggestion that she see Dr. Blanchard. Marsha reassured her that she only wanted the best for her. Dr. Blanchard was experienced, warm, and perceptive. She could help Janice.

Reluctantly, Janice has carried the doctor's crumpled pink card around in her wallet for weeks, half embarrassed that she even thinks about talking to anyone about her private life. Just admitting that she can't deal with this breakup by herself is devastating. In addition to getting over Tom, she has to feel like a wimp. Strong women make it—and they make it on their own, she chides herself.

Janice is a smart woman. She has pitched proposals to everyone from CEOs of major corporations to proprietors of mom-and-pop outfits. She's poised under pressure, her presentations to prospective clients are seamless, and her performance reviews stellar. She always outdistances the others in sales and customer satisfaction. Flawless performance and business finesse are Janice's guiding principles. She's the heart of diplomacy and fiercely protective of the interests of her clients. She knows her success depends on theirs.

Janice rides the elevator skyward to Dr. Blanchard's office, reminding herself that she can handle anyone and that seeing a psychologist is something a lot of women do. Going into therapy does not make her some kind of nutcase.

Dr. Blanchard's waiting room is pleasantly appointed—sea-foam green and peach sofas, mahogany furniture, brass lamps. This seems normal enough. Soothing colors and quiet music—nothing too threatening so far. So why does she wish she was on the other side of the world?

Dr. Blanchard is prompt. She clips down the short hallway to fetch Janice, seats herself in a large chair opposite Janice's, and smiles warmly. At fifty-seven, Dr. Blanchard has that "older woman" elegance. She's slender, fit, tanned, and completely white head-ed. Obviously a woman who takes weekends off. And I bet she even has time for tennis during the week, Janice muses sourly.

All of a sudden, Janice realizes the moment of truth has arrived. She speaks frankly. She needs all her business confidence to usher her through this one. She wants to be clear, forthright, and under control. That's what plays in her head. But all she hears herself say is, "He left me. He really left me . . . and there's nothing I can do to bring him back." The words come out in a wail of tears.

Dr. Blanchard nods and waits. "Obviously," she reflects to Janice, "this ending has been quite painful for you." More tears and more gulps as Janice tries to regain control of her feelings. She has not admitted to anyone the constant sadness she feels—every day, every minute. When she sleeps, she dreams about Tom. Even things she used to do for fun—hiking, eat-ing out, exercising—seem bland and one dimension-al. She's depressed, and Dr. Blanchard seems to understand the need to stay out of her way as she vents and begins to release the emotions that are strangling her. She is so sick of feeling this way. She wants her life back.

CHAPTER 5

Are You a Victim
of FESS?

*T*O HELP YOU to better understand FESS, I want
to introduce you to a typical client. "Susan" is a composite of many of my clients. The identifying variables of
her life have been altered to protect confidentiality, but her
experiences are real, and her situation is typical of many of the
patients I have seen over the last ten years.

Susan was born in Chicago in 1950, the firstborn child of
a working-class Italian family. Her mother had two stillbirths
before Susan, and two more live baby girls after Susan.
Susan's family lived and worked in their close-knit neighborhood. Her father ran a small grocery store. Her mother
worked there part-time and took in sewing on the side. Early
on in life, Susan learned the value of hard work, long hours,
and punctuality.

Susan was familiar with the concept of customer service.
She watched her mother and father work in the store, and she

understood that her own needs were always secondary to pleasing others. When Susan was nine years old, her father asked her to work in the store stocking the shelves. She didn't get along well with her father. He was gruff and cared little about her feelings, yet she found herself identifying strongly with him since he was the most powerful person in the family.

Susan's father was delighted to discover that Susan had a gift for retailing. He was proud of her ability to interact with customers and to juggle a number of different mental tasks at once, keeping up with her stocking while assisting customers and handling money. Prior to working in the store, Susan had been invisible to her father. Now that she worked side by side with him and performed well in his world, he gave her additional emotional support. But she was acutely aware that his attention was closely tied to her performance and perfection.

Susan's family was Catholic, and at home the parental roles were traditional and patriarchal. Her father ruled the roost; her mother was passive and secondary. Susan learned that to gain any power, you had to be a male. From her mother Susan learned to get along with other people. Her mother was nurturing and a peacemaker who would never challenge Susan's father. Later, the effects of these parental roles would be highly visible in Susan's life. Her mother's role as nurturer and her unconditional love, juxtaposed with her father's conditional attention, would characterize Susan's own internal struggles.

We all tend to "internalize" our parents. Their personalities become our own internal prescriptions. As grown-ups, the internal voices that criticize or encourage us are the voices of our parents telling us what we are supposed to be. For Susan, and for many other executive women who grew up with passive mothers, there was an innate role conflict, with one voice saying she should be like Mom and raise a family and stay home, while another said she should continue being more like Dad.

For these women, the characteristics of black-and-white, nonemotional thinking, being a perfectionist, and being aggressive are all gleaned from their fathers. Being this way makes them feel powerful, in control, and safe. When they become feminine or maternal, they more closely resemble their mothers. Immediately they believe they must relinquish power. They feel out of control, in danger. The choice to them is between full control and no control. It is their own internal images that cause this division.

Often I tell patients that their parents are "riding around in their heads," talking to them nonstop. If your actions clash with what your parent would say or do, it results in internal anxiety and strife, and you tend to think and feel you are a bad person, whether it is true or not. I am convinced that this is especially true of women in executive positions who go to extraordinary lengths to perform. That drive comes from those powerful fathers. Because these executive women are living alternative lifestyles, the magnitude of the parental role clash is bigger for them than for almost anyone else in our society.

Performance equals love

BECAUSE SHE PUT in such long hours in the family business, Susan never felt she had the freedom to participate in school activities. She had to perform well both in school and on the job to earn her father's love and attention. She was never editor of the yearbook or president of the student council. She was smart enough, well liked, and had excellent grades, but she simply didn't have time. Teachers called Susan "intense." And they worried that she didn't have time for a social life and was always striving to do better and better in school. This lack of social experience would greatly influence Susan's adult development.

Susan's hard work paid off, and she earned an academic scholarship to Loyola, a good Jesuit School; this pleased her dad. At Loyola, she majored in business and finance—a rarity for a woman in 1968. Susan was planning to take over the family business someday and saw the value in gaining financial skill. But in her senior year, Susan suffered a great blow to her self-esteem when she learned that her father had other plans for the store. He brought in one of her cousins, a boy younger than Susan, whom he planned to train to take over someday. When her father retired with heart problems that year and left the cousin in charge, rather than calling for Susan's help, she fell apart.

Blocked from her source of gratification—the career she had chosen—Susan felt she had no identity. With no way to earn her father's love, she felt she was left with nothing. The family business was closely tied with Susan's own good feelings about herself; with this door closed to her, she felt she had no way to prove herself to her father.

Susan developed a full-blown clinical depression. For the first time in her life, she could not perform. She couldn't get out of bed to make it to class. She wasn't turning in school papers. She was tearful, withdrawn, and overwhelmed with feelings of worthlessness. She began to think about suicide. She already felt like she had ceased to exist, so the prospect of death offered comfort, a way of ending the pain. But deep inside Susan was resilient, a characteristic of FESS women. Her roommate dragged her to the campus mental health clinic. She got help, pulled herself together, and made it to graduation, with her family never the wiser.

> Susan developed a full-blown clinical depression. For the first time in her life, she could not perform.

Holding on to anger

THE NEXT YEAR, 1971, Susan attended graduate school at Boston College. She was still fragile, but she held on to her anger with her father, and that anger became a sustaining force in her life. Susan was more driven than ever and seethed with an "I'll show you" attitude. She received no financial support from her parents. Still interested in the retail world, Susan worked a full-time job in a Boston department store and still pulled high grades. Early on, she caught the eye of a professor who helped set her up with internships in some of the major retail corporations in Boston.

Susan became a buyer, a safe and traditional position for a woman in the early seventies. She planned to learn the business from the ground up, using the philosophy she learned so well from her father. By age twenty-five, Susan was coming along well professionally. She put her career first and found there was a lot of support for women in her position. She had come into her own during the Golden Age of the women's movement. So even though Susan had little support from her family for choosing a career over a traditional family role, she had the women's movement staunchly behind her.

Choosing the wrong man

TYPICAL OF SO MANY WOMEN in this group, Susan chose a man who was a stark contrast to her father. Dan was someone nice, warm, and affectionate, and he was not nearly as driven as she was. This man filled the role in her adult life that her mother occupied when Susan was growing up—that of all-giving nurturer. In this relationship, Susan spent most of her energy pushing Dan further and faster than he wanted to go in his career. Still, they married. Susan was thirty-one and she continued to work her eighty-hour weeks, spending very little time at home.

From the beginning, Susan worked to sabotage the relationship. Dan offered her more intimacy than she could stand. He wanted to build a life to share with her—a concept completely alien to Susan. The nicer he was, the more anxious she became. Within a few short years, she couldn't stand it any longer, so she began to emasculate him, criticizing him for his lack of ambition. Dan was an accountant, and Susan constantly harped on him that he was not aggressive enough, that he was being used by his company, and that he was not getting what he deserved. Understandably, Dan got tired of the pushing and wanted out of the relationship. Susan, who had been oblivious to his feelings all along, reacted with pain and confusion. Dan wanted an intimate relationship, and Susan's long hours, their lack of a social life, and countless frozen dinners, never added up to a marriage for him. To Susan, the marriage was just a pit stop between business trips.

When Dan finally left, after Susan had a blatant affair with a co-worker, Susan was actually relieved. There was no one invading her psychological space anymore, which is exactly the way she liked it. Unfortunately, during her brief affair she discovered a pathological pattern that appealed to her. With an affair she could have pseudo-intimacy, sleep with a variety of men, fly off to see them for an exciting weekend, and avoid all of the demands of an ongoing commitment. She rationalized this pattern of relationships by telling herself that with the job demands she had, she just didn't have time to be in an intimate, ongoing relationship.

For the next ten years, Susan continued in this pattern of brief relationships while she excelled and was rewarded with promotions at work. At forty-five, she was given her own store to manage—the first woman in her corporation to be given this power and responsibility. All of the pieces were in place for Susan to have a major debilitating episode of FESS, exhibiting all eight characteristics of the syndrome:

> From the beginning, Susan worked to sabotage the relationship. Dan offered her more intimacy than she could stand....With an affair she could have pseudo-intimacy, sleep with a variety of men, fly off to see them for an exciting weekend, and avoid all of the demands of an ongoing commitment.

1. Perfectionism

Susan's behavior was typical of the "I am what I do" syndrome that is present in virtually every executive client I see. She expected the best—from herself and from everyone around her. How Susan felt about herself was contingent on how she performed at work. She was more apt to be described by people at work as hardworking than as a perfectionist, because she was so eager to keep everyone happy that she didn't impose her standards upon the people around her. She may not have respected co-workers who did not share her work ethic, but she tended to hold back from pointing this out until the resentment built. When it reached a boiling point, Susan exploded, and her associates looked at each other in disbelief, not understanding why something so small caused such a large reaction. Most of the time, however, her department worked well—after all, it was all an extension of Susan.

2. Can't Take A Compliment

Despite her confident exterior, Susan had a self-esteem problem. Women who suffer from FESS have an inability to fully integrate positive feedback. They can't intellectually or emotionally acknowledge that they have done something well. One client told me that getting positive feedback didn't make her feel good. She had difficulty believing that the other person was sincere. She was sure they had a hidden agenda and meant to mislead her.

Like other FESS women, Susan was uncomfortable with positive feedback, whether it came during a job review or from clients. She had a host of disclaimers ready, her favorite being to ascribe her great performance to luck. She had good people around her, the economy was good in the region—that's why her store was number one in the chain. Susan didn't know how to nurture herself, just as she didn't know how to nurture other people.

3. They Would Rather Be At Work

Like most FESS victims, working and performing were far more comfortable for Susan than taking time out to relax. To really relax, Susan would have to slow down, and slowing down always felt like defeat. Surrendering her ambition, even on a vacation, would make her wild. To feel okay, FESS women have to keep marching. These women feel the need to quantify their leisure time in the same bottom-line way they do their work time—at the end of the vacation, just as in at the end of each day, they want to have something to show for their time and effort.

Susan hated weekends because she had to focus on herself; she had to *feel* her emotions. Being in retail, she had a good excuse to go to the office on weekends. If she was not at the office, she might be off on a trip with one of her boyfriends, but you wouldn't find her networking with other women or spending time with her family. Sunday was the worst day of the week for her, a quiet day with no distractions to keep her from feeling alone. She usually passed the time doing paperwork she had brought home from the office or reading up on trends in the industry.

4. Split Personality

Susan felt like two different women. She was appropriately assertive, creative, and professional at work. In contrast, Susan's personal life had deteriorated. She was deeply disappointed in herself for letting things go this far. She felt things had spiraled out of control, beyond repair. Susan felt hopeless.

Like most FESS women, Susan's personal life was "in the dumps." Over and over these women seek out "serial mates," only to sabotage the relationship as the intimacy increases. They function in their personal lives in ways they wouldn't tolerate in their professional lives. At work, they are effective, master manipulators who work well with others toward a common goal. In their personal relationships with men, they balance on a seesaw of emotion and feel out of control if a man gets too close.

5. Can't Think Pink

Susan is typical of the FESS woman who feels cut off from her feminine side to the point that she views femininity in a negative light and avoids any expressions that might be viewed as peculiarly feminine. Since childhood, she has strongly identified with masculine characteristics.

The less Susan had to do with her intuitive, nurturing side, the better she felt. She did not mentor other people at work because such behavior would be too much like the behavior she did not respect in her mother. She overemphasized her own independence because she was scared to death of her own needs for belonging and relying on others. Again, any softness or caring meant only a lack of control to Susan. If she let down her guard, she was afraid she would lose her edge. Without this advantage, she would be unable to excel.

6. Work As Escape

Susan's work was her solace, and she often used it as an escape to soothe self-doubts and anxieties. She thought if she just worked harder, everything would get better and the problems at home would go away. Whenever Susan felt she was losing control, she went to the office. There she knew and controlled the environment, so she felt safe.

7. Performance Equals Love

Susan's relationship with her parents was completely performance driven—a classic FESS woman's parental relationship. She never felt unconditional love from her father. Typically, Susan had unresolved issues with her father. She had never talked with him about his giving the store to her cousin. If asked, she'd say her relationship with her parents was fine. She called them on birthdays, Mother's Day, and Father's Day, and she went home for holidays when work allowed (which was seldom). Susan wanted to be perfect, so her performance-driven parental relationships were a can of worms best avoided.

8. Fear Of Intimacy

Susan's personal life was fraught with intimacy difficulties. FESS women find intimacy difficult because of the lack of structure in personal relationships as compared to professional ones. Within the context of work, rules and expectations are structured and clear, so it's easier for these women to know what to do to feel good about themselves. In a relationship, there are no rules or boundaries, making it harder to know how to act and how to feel. FESS women often have marriages with no real intimacy or affairs that can be cut off when they get too close.

One of Susan's favorite lines was "I can't do relationships." She had opted out of them at this point in her career—well on her way to CFO. Yet, when a career crisis propelled her into a depression, she changed her mind about her current pseudo-relationship fling. Blocked from getting what she needed at work to feel good about herself, she actually began to care about the person she was sleeping with. As she developed these tender feelings, the emotional investment made her feel anxious and vulnerable, so she began to sabotage the relationship. Going away to the islands for the weekend, she got drunk on the plane and acted like a total jerk, forcing him to give her an ultimatum.

Women do not have to display all of the above characteristics to qualify for the FESS diagnosis. However, their typical behavior usually includes at least four of them. Different variants of FESS may be determined by the nature of parental relationships as well as the kinds of quirks of fate that may alter a woman's life course in different ways.

Loss of perspective

WHEN HER LIFE BEGAN to fall apart, Susan completely lost her perspective. She was a black-and-white thinker. In her world, she was only as good as her last deal or her last promotion. Having been passed over for a promotion, she expected the worst—her days were numbered. Of course, this was

ridiculous. Susan was a valuable employee and her performance had been nothing but excellent, but she had no
patience. Stripped of her chance at the brass ring she felt
deflated and devastated. She could not see that she only needed to bide her time until she got another opportunity for promotion.

Patience is not a virtue for FESS women.
Throughout their careers, they have been
positively reinforced for their impatience.
They have gotten raises and bonuses because
they are impatient and driven. Patience characterizes giving up control—something they
cannot tolerate.

> Patience is not a virtue
> for FESS women.
> They have gotten raises
> and bonuses because they
> are impatient and driven.
> Patience characterizes
> giving up control—
> something
> they cannot tolerate.

Extent of debilitation

FOR THE SECOND TIME in her life, Susan
had a full-blown clinical depression with all of the icing. Her
productivity at work suffered. She withdrew from social contact because she feared she was losing her edge, and her fears
became a self-fulfilling prophecy. Depression clouded Susan's
thinking; she was unable to concentrate. Her fall was a gradual one because Susan had excellent coping skills. Her tremendous ego had been a source of strength. Despite her best
efforts, Susan's performance began to erode.

Unable to sleep, Susan lived with constant feelings of
dread and despair. For the first time in her life she began to
gain weight, having given up her exercise program because she
no longer had the energy for it.

Susan's job performance was compromised, but she was far from inadequate. Her personal life, however, was a disaster. She was subservient to her new long-distance boyfriend, and exhibited behaviors with him that would be unfamiliar to anyone who knew her professionally. Finally, he rejected her. She was alone, without a network of friends, personal or professional.

Like many women with FESS, Susan drank to excess. While she was not a true alcoholic, she drank too much wine, using it as a calming agent. In high-pressure business situations, a drink or two more than normal usually took the edge off. Drinking contributed to her depression, but she didn't want to give it up. She drank more and enjoyed it less.

Susan's fatigue and loss of energy became more pronounced. She had a cold off and on for months and couldn't seem to get rid of it, so she finally made an appointment with her internist to discuss her symptoms. Now mature and a seasoned professional, Susan didn't fall apart as she had in college. Instead, she saw a psychologist recommended by her internist to begin to work toward recovery.

Susan's struggles, unfortunately, are all too common among the victims of FESS.

CHAPTER 6

Stress and the
Working Woman:
Understanding the FESS Study

THE FESS STUDY was motivated by a desire to validate my clinical findings about FESS and to determine to what extent FESS is a problem in American society. Our findings mimicked what I've seen in my practice with executive women.

Information concerning the questionnaires used and statistical analyses performed for this study can be found in appendix 2 and appendix 3. The present chapter will focus on the basic conclusions derived from the results of the FESS study.

Characteristics of the FESS study sample

THE EIGHTY-SEVEN WOMEN in our sample averaged forty-two years of age. Sixty-eight percent of these women were married, 21 percent were divorced, 10 percent had never been married, and 1 percent were widowed. Women with no children comprised 41 percent of the sample, 17 percent of the women had one child, 35 percent had two children, and 2 percent had between three and five children. (The remaining 5 percent of mothers did not specify their number of children.) When we asked these executives about their home life, 27 percent said that they were "happy and fulfilled"; 39 percent said that they were "satisfied"; 14 percent said that they were "okay but troubled"; 4 percent said that they had "unstable and troubled" marital relationships; and 2 percent said that their marriages were "unhappy." (The rest of the subjects didn't specify a response to this item.) Approximately 60 percent of the women claimed they had never had an extramarital affair, while 35 percent admitted to having an affair in the past, and 5 percent admitted that they were having an affair at present.

On average, the FESS study executives worked about fifty-three hours per week, had been with their present company about fifteen years, and had had their last promotion about two years earlier. Not surprisingly, about 75 percent of the sample worked in companies where women were in the minority.

About 47 percent of the women asserted that their yearly salary was at or above $75,000. Twenty-three percent of the sample claimed they earned $100,000 or more per year. Fully 71 percent of the sample maintained that they had a higher yearly salary than their mates'; 61 percent of the sample indicated this difference was $10,000 or more per year.

Only 1 percent of the women who participated in the FESS study were the CEOs of their companies; 15 percent described themselves simply as "executives"; 41 percent said they were in "upper management"; 30 percent maintained they were in "middle management"; and 2 percent described themselves as "lower management." (Eleven percent asserted "other," which included independent consultants and small business owners.)

The FESS study executives were a highly educated, dynamic group of women. About 13 percent held a graduate degree, 46 percent earned a bachelor's degree, 10 percent held an associate's degree, 24 percent had high school diplomas and some college credit, and 2 percent had high school diplomas only.

Leisure time was one luxury that many executive women did not have—especially when compared to their mates. Fully 41 percent of the FESS study executives said that their mates had ten hours or more leisure time than they did per week, and another 18 percent said their mates had between five and ten hours more leisure time per week. These findings offer support for Arlie Hochschild's landmark study described in her book, *The Second Shift*. It has been five years since these data were published, and women are still experiencing a substantial "leisure gap." Tragically, this gap exists even at the executive level in marriages where women are outearning their husbands.

For those executives who had children, parenting responsibilities were another reason for a lack of leisure time. Over 50

The FESS study executives were a highly educated, dynamic group of women. About 13 percent held a graduate degree, 46 percent earned a bachelor's degree, 10 percent held an associate's degree, 24 percent had high school diplomas and some college credit, and 2 percent had high school diplomas only.

percent of the married executive mothers asserted they did more of the parenting than their spouses. Once again, even when women advanced to powerful positions outside the home and earned a larger salary than their husbands, the traditional division of parenting labor prevailed. Women might have broken barriers to their success in the work world, but they have fallen far short of such breakthroughs in their marriages. The major burden of child rearing still falls on the woman.

Sexual harassment was not an issue of great concern for these women. This finding might indicate that their being in positions of power helped to discourage this activity in men. In fact, almost half of the women in the sample did not believe they had ever been sexually harassed. Less than one out of five women in the sample had ever been traumatized by sexual harassment. The interviews I conducted with those who had been harassed afforded many of these women an opportunity to describe their early experiences. They were convinced that their lack of power had left them vulnerable in a sexist system. As one woman said, "I would never let that guy get away with it now. . . . I'd see him in court."

Personality and emotional life data

THE FESS STUDY DATA provided a reasonably clear picture of the overall emotional health of our sample. As a group, they seemed as healthy as the average American woman, and appeared to possess average amounts of emotional resources that enable women to cope with stress successfully. However, the FESS study executives employed certain kinds of specific coping strategies for resolving stressful situations that worked more effectively than the typical strategies of the average women. The women in our sample placed far more emphasis than the average women on behavioral restraint and emotional control. They avoided impulsive displays of thought and emotion, preferring to think through possible solutions. They tried to understand their suffering and adversity in terms of what they learned and how they grew from these experiences. They worked hard to develop a step-by-step problem-solving plan and bent all efforts to following this plan exactly. The FESS study executives also actively sought out the advice and reassurance of friends and family members. These women placed a much stronger emphasis on these particular coping strategies than was found with the average American women. In addition, they were more flexible and more apt to try several different strategies to identify the best solution.

The FESS study sample displayed an extremely high degree of Type A behavior, which research has linked with coronary heart disease. These women felt constantly pressured and were more compulsively driven than the average American woman. Most of these women seemed like workaholics. They also exhibited such other Type A characteristics as impatience, competitiveness, and high-handedness at work. These women were "gunners." They were classified as Type A more frequently than most men! The following case study describes one such woman:

You'll never find Annabeth at home in the evenings. She's hard at work at the firm, alone on the fifty-fifth floor. If you really want to talk to her, you have to beep her because the firm switchboard closes down at 6:00 P.M. on weekdays. Even then, unless you indicate that your message is urgent, Annabeth is not likely to call you back. She'll never be straight about blowing you off but will mutter some excuse about a malfunction in her beeper. It's true. Annabeth is a workaholic—a classic Type A.

In the last year, Annabeth's performance has comfortably outstripped all of the firm's predictions. She has excelled far beyond expectation. Self-disciplined and direct, she can be hard to deal with sometimes because she's so impatient. Occasionally, she loses sight of the big picture because she's so driven and focused. She's fond of saying to her staff, as they follow her brisk steps down the stairwell, that she never asks anyone to do anything she's not willing to do herself. Her support staff remains chronically bewildered as she heaps on the work. Burnout is a big risk for anybody who works for Annabeth. She has gone through six secretaries in two years. People tend to bail out before their lives fall apart. After all, they don't want to end up like Annabeth.

Annabeth has trouble seeing the other person's point of view when she's in a hurry. She forgets about their feelings. She wants the job done when she tells them. No excuses and no delays. Numerous partners have tried to broach the subject with her but to no avail. Annabeth always retorts that she has standards and needs tough people to meet them. After awhile, most of her colleagues learn to avoid the subject of staff relations with her. The bottom line is always met. Annabeth is a producer and, as a result, enjoys an invisible but potent immunity from mundane firm rules. Annabeth is in a league of her own—all alone.

Annabeth typifies one of the most striking findings of our study—the pronounced differences between the FESS study women and average American women in sexual role identification. This involved the degree to which an individual identified with and displayed characteristics that were stereotypically viewed as masculine versus feminine in American society. It was *not* related to sexual orientation, but emphasized traits that were routinely apparent in everyday living. Most people have some combination of masculine and feminine characteristics, although many people strongly identify with and personify one set of sex role characteristics or the other. Surprisingly, the *majority* of the FESS study women displayed a predominantly masculine role identification. Less than one out of ten women in the group displayed a higher degree of feminine role identification.

What does all of this mean? Our sample had discovered that to survive in a man's world, they would have to become more like men. Assertive, independent, dominant, and self-confident, these women found that they could be everything their male counterparts were. They could beat men at their own game. This finding makes a strong statement about what it takes for a woman to succeed in corporate America today.

**F
E
S
S**

The FESS study women consistently displayed high levels of self-esteem, surpassing the minimum level of high self-esteem that is reached by only one out of four average American women. It is possible that a woman's pursuit of a fulfilling career is central to the development of high self-esteem.

Secrets of the most successful female executives

THE NEXT SECTION of the study attempted to isolate those female executives who were the most successful at coping effectively with stressful situations. These women minimized any symptoms of emotional distress and rose in the ranks of an American corporate structure that is still male dominated and favors the success of male executives. How did these women do it? These successful executives were the least likely to suffer from the Female Executive Stress Syndrome, and their methods might contain curative elements for those women who do suffer from FESS.

The study found that approximately 50 percent of the women displayed average levels of stress symptoms, approximately 33 percent of the women were very healthy—far above the norm—and about 17 percent of the women probably suffered from FESS.

The average group of women experience some stress, and they periodically face ups and downs and struggles in their

> The study found that approximately 50 percent of the women displayed average levels of stress symptoms, approximately 33 percent of the women were very healthy—far above the norm—and about 17 percent of the women probably suffered from FESS.

working environment that often exacerbate stress. This seems to be the norm for all of us. This group has a few symptoms of FESS but does not suffer from the full-blown syndrome. Like many people, they may be symptomatic, but also may never set foot in a psychologist's office. Most importantly, though, stress keeps these women from functioning at their optimal level. It keeps them from reaching their full "fire power." They could benefit from a variety of efforts to reduce their stress—from private therapy to company seminars that address how to better cope with stress at work and at home. Businesses would be far more productive if everyone were functioning at the highest levels of health and vigor, and coping well with stress. The secrets to functioning well can be learned by anyone, and could be of great use in corporate America.

In my clinical practice, I have observed that a small percentage of the women who come to me exhibit all of the symptoms of FESS. These women make up between 2 and 5 percent of my practice, and they may be in therapy for as long as three years before they recover from the syndrome. Similar to what we learned in the study, far more of my patients exhibit half or more of the FESS symptoms. They are the patients who are not in therapy very long—often only six months. They work hard and recover quickly, and they are very healthy when they leave. The most successful and effective female executives usually don't come to my office unless fate is extremely unkind to them in ways that they literally cannot control. Again, there is a pattern of rapid recovery and ultimate success.

Perhaps the most exciting result of the FESS study is the discovery of two clusters of women who are healthy, happy, and functioning far better than anyone would have predicted. These women are at the top of their game. As a psychologist who sees women struggling to recover from problems, I take great pleasure in studying and writing about these two superlative groups and sharing their secrets for success. We can all learn from their wisdom.

Statistical analyses formed each group by clustering together subjects who were highly similar on several different levels. These two "healthy" clusters shared more characteristics with each other than they did with the remaining heterogeneous pool of subjects. In other words, healthy women "hang together."

The healthiest group were the oldest, on average, of the three groups in the sample, and, not surprisingly, had the largest average number of years with their present companies. I decided to call them the "Seasoned Executives." The second healthy group were the youngest on average and had fewer years with their company than the Seasoned Executives. I called this group the "Young Turks" because they appeared to be ambitious, hard driving, and highly successful. The large remaining group was called the "Stressed Group" because they clearly were less successful and more stressed than the two healthy groups.

Just as I have learned so much from my executive patients, I have learned from these women ways to a more efficient, happier, healthier life. Now you can learn how to climb to the top with your sanity and health intact.

The Seasoned Executives

F E S S

THIS GROUP had an average age of just over forty-four years and had been with their present companies just over twenty years. They had the most years of seniority when compared with the others. This finding suggests that the Seasoned Executives have been more adaptive in the corporate environment and more successful at reaping the rewards of their own abilities and health than the rest of the women in the study. More than nine out of ten Seasoned Executives were married, and over half of this group had children. In addition, more than half of this group had yearly salaries above $75,000, with more than 90 percent of the married members of the Seasoned Executives' salaries exceeding their mates' by at least $10,000 per year. Remarkably, more than nine out of ten married Seasoned Executives asserted that they were happy and fulfilled in their marriages. These women had been loyal to their marriage vows—less than one out of five Seasoned Executives admitted to ever having an extramarital affair. This personal and professional success was even more remarkable given that many couples would have problems if the women earned a larger salary than the men. These women were able to blend power with femininity and intimacy.

The Seasoned Executives reported the fewest problems in their happiness with their careers, their sexual relationships,

> The Seasoned Executives reported the fewest problems in their happiness with their careers, their sexual relationships, their co-worker relationships, and their parental relationships. These women reported the lowest overall levels of stress in their lives in comparison to our entire sample.

their co-worker relationships, and their parental relationships. They had the second lowest levels of stress from sexual discrimination and burnout. These women reported the lowest overall levels of stress in their lives in comparison to our entire sample. This group also reported the lowest levels of depression, fatigue, confusion, and anger, and the highest levels of vigor and energy. They were self-confident and balanced. The Seasoned Executives easily had the lowest overall levels of emotional distress.

How did they manage to cope so well? They were the most successful of all groups at establishing and maintaining meaningful friendships that could be sources of strength and support in times of stress. They did the best job of any group in restraining and controlling their feelings and behavior, avoiding impulsive displays of thought and emotion, waiting until they could think through possible solutions. When necessary, they were more apt to seek safe and supportive places in which to vent their negative feelings. These women were dedicated exercisers and viewed physical activity as stress reducing. In general, the Seasoned Executives were the most flexible and employed the widest range of coping strategies. If they had a problem, they found a good solution. They had good instincts and used them, so they landed on their feet.

The Seasoned Executives also *avoided* certain types of coping strategies more than other study groups. They were the least likely of all groups to withdraw from stressful circumstances and engage in fantasy. They were less likely to accept blame and then react by making unnecessary amends to others. They also were less likely to be aggressively confrontive.

These women were deliberate, effective, and calculating. They thought an issue through before they took action.

One of the most important findings concerning the Seasoned Executives involved the nature of their sexual role identification. Over half of this group displayed high levels of identification with *both* masculine and feminine characteristics. Those who did not fit this category were more masculine in their identification. A strong and balanced identification with both masculine and feminine characteristics was typical of this most successful and happiest of the study groups.

The Young Turks

THE YOUNG TURKS comprised 18 percent of the study group. This was the youngest group in the sample, with an average age of just under forty years. In spite of their youth, they had the second-highest average career length with their present companies. This indicates that the Young Turks have been highly effective in the corporate environment in a comparatively short amount of time, with many of them probably spending their entire careers with one company.

Just over two-thirds of this group were married, and about two out of five group members had children. These women were big earners. Exactly half of this group had yearly salaries above $75,000, and about two-thirds of the married members of the Young Turks had salaries that exceeded their mates'. (In most cases this difference was at least $10,000 per year.) All of the married group members asserted that they were happy and fulfilled in their marriages. For the entire Young Turks group,

F
E
S
S

three out of five asserted that they had never had an extramarital affair. Twenty-seven percent said they had had an extramarital affair in the past, and 13 percent said they presently were involved in an affair. As a group, the Young Turks were not as apparently successful as the Seasoned Executives in sustaining both impressive careers and happy personal lives.

The Young Turks reported the lowest overall levels of stress from sexual discrimination and job burnout. Despite less fulfilling marriages, their overall levels of stress were only slightly higher than that measured for the Seasoned Executives.

Some of the Young Turks showed patterns reminiscent of the Seasoned Executives, possibly indicating an earlier incarnation of what will be the next group of Seasoned Executives.

The Young Turks reported somewhat more stress than did the Seasoned Executives in relation to career satisfaction, their sexual relationships, their co-worker relationships, and their parental relationships. The differences between this group and the Seasoned Executives were most pronounced in their co-worker relationships, where the stress levels of the Young Turks actually were closer to the stress levels of the Stressed Group. The Young Turks were much closer to the Seasoned Executives on the remaining dimensions.

The Young Turks reported the lowest overall levels of stress from sexual discrimination and job burnout. Despite less fulfilling marriages, their overall levels of stress were only slightly higher than that measured for the Seasoned Executives. They had a slightly lower level of anxiety and they displayed the second lowest levels of depression, fatigue, confusion, and anger. The Young Turks' level of vigor and energy was more similar to the low-energy Stressed Group, and was much lower than the energy level of the Seasoned Executives. These women are driven and tired.

The overall level of emotional distress symptoms displayed by the Young Turks fell about halfway between the other two groups. In essence, the Young Turks were not as successful as the Seasoned Executives in coping with stressful situations, but they were much more successful in this task than were members of the Stressed Group. In addition, they showed higher levels of vigor and lower levels of emotional distress than the average American woman.

The Young Turks employed a somewhat different set of coping strategies than the Seasoned Executives, with a reasonable amount of success. In contrast to the Seasoned Executives, the Young Turks were the least likely of all groups to establish and maintain networks of meaningful relationships that they could turn to for strength and support in times of stress. They were less likely than other study groups to practice restraint and more likely to shoot from the hip, with occasional disastrous consequences. They were almost as likely as the Stressed Group to withdraw from stress and retreat into a fantasy and denial. By contrast, the Seasoned Executives almost completely avoided withdrawing since it did not promote positive change. They only expended energy if it was productive. These differences in coping strategies may explain, in part, why the Young Turks were not as successful as the Seasoned Executives in coping with stressful situations and minimizing emotional distress.

Although some differences were evident, the Young Turks shared several of the coping strategies used by the Seasoned Executives. They were almost as likely as the Seasoned Executives to turn to trusted friends to talk about their feelings. And the Young Turks were the most likely of all study groups to pursue exercise and other health-promoting behaviors to reduce stress. They were the least likely to accept blame for a problem and then react by making amends with others.

The Young Turks bring a lot to the table, but still finish second in effective coping when compared to the Seasoned Executives.

One striking finding with the Young Turks was the nature of their sexual role identification. Four out of five Young Turks displayed the highest average of all study groups for level of identification with masculine characteristics. These women conceptualized themselves as being far more driven, domineering, and forceful than most women. They prided themselves on their self-sufficiency and their strength. Their lack of identification with feminine characteristics could help explain why the Young Turks were less flexible and adaptive in their coping strategies than were the Seasoned Executives.

The road to success

OVERALL, the FESS study reveals that executive women function at dramatically different levels psychologically. The Seasoned Executives offer us a picture of working women in full bloom. They have it all—a sense of self that is rich and cohesive—and they know it. They are fully evolved women, both internally and externally.

The Young Turks are a work in progress. They are sitting firmly in the saddle but need to learn that flexibility, intuition, and a strong awareness of one's emotions are valuable assets in the corporate world. They have some things to learn but are on the right path.

The Stressed Group presents a variegated view of the challenges facing executive women. As with the Young Turks, and many of us, they have yet to fully integrate their intellectual and emotional sides to reach maximum effectiveness. They are far more vulnerable to stress because they do not utilize the good coping skills of the Young Turks or the superior strategies of the Seasoned Executives. It is fair to conclude that this group, as contrasted to the Seasoned Executives and the Young Turks, have the most psychological work yet to do. The Stressed Group may be representative of the executive women who struggle the most in the American patriarchy. And they are still learning, evolving, and searching for improved strategies for coping in a man's world.

CHAPTER 7

Successful Strategies
for Coping with FESS

THE MOST GRATIFYING PART of the FESS study is being able to share the proven coping strategies for success used by the executives who have made it to the top and who remain solid and healthy and happy. These ten coping strategies form a blueprint for success and an antidote for FESS that all women can use:

Coping strategies—ten steps to success

1. **Form strong friendships and social networks.**
2. **Cultivate your ability to appropriately express a wide range of emotions.**
3. **Broaden your personality to include both "female" and "male" characteristics.**
4. **Exercise vigorously on a regular basis.**
5. **Avoid self-blaming.**

F
E
S
S

6. **Nurture and guard your self-esteem.**

7. **Pursue a strong commitment to your profession or your company.**

8. **Minimize an aggressive, confrontive style of problem solving.**

9. **Embrace a calculated, measured style of problem solving.**

10. **Take an action-oriented approach to life.**

Following is a full discussion of each of these strategies with examples to help you start using these coping skills immediately in your everyday life.

Form strong friendships and social networks

SUCCESSFUL EXECUTIVES in the FESS study place a high value on friendship, and are less stressed as a result. They form "families of friends" and invest time in their social networks; this time is repaid with effective insulation that acts as a barrier to stress.

We are no longer in the second grade, when a friend was someone we joined at the hip who fulfilled our every social need. As adults, women need several true friends who can form a mutual support system, be a resource for venting problems, and people with whom to relax.

Often women with FESS expect their friends to be all things to them. I try to emphasize that they need to be tolerant, to expect the disappointments that will naturally come with any close friendship. Friends, even the best of friends, will occasionally let you down. They are only human. But FESS women tend to back off too quickly when they've been let down. They dismiss people as if they've fired them for poor job performance. I stress that they need to give these friends another chance. Remember, friendship is a gradual process, filled with ups and downs.

I tell my FESS patients that they shouldn't overreact when someone disappoints them. Instead, pay attention—analyze the situation. Was this a stray act that may have been caused by other factors in their friend's life? I stress the need for observation to keep these women from getting in a position where they are wasting their time and being used. Keen observational skills also may help them avoid giving up too soon on a new but promising relationship.

> As adults, women need several true friends who can form a mutual support system, be a resource for venting problems, and people with whom to relax.

A lawyer friend of mine once said that everything a person does tells you something about them. Assemble a mosaic of the people you choose as friends—every little piece builds a pattern. You can do this fairly quickly for everyone you meet if you develop an acute way of thinking about and listening to what happens.

I do think executives need to have friendships with women who have been in their world and stood in their shoes. Friends need to be able to know what you are dealing with on some level. Find a common ground, a point of connection. And be flexible—you can have different friends who serve different needs.

F
E
S
S

   Pursue honesty in your friendships. You need to have the ability to be blunt with one another if venting and feedback are to be beneficial. If you can only sustain social chatter, the friendship is not the type of support system needed to help you with the stress you face in your life.

   Friendship offers tremendous benefits. The feeling of being understood is priceless. It validates your experience and decreases the isolation that comes with a fast-paced world. Friends can help you put your problems in perspective and realize that we are all interrelated—that your problems are similar to everybody else's. Most importantly, talking with good friends about what is going on in your life helps you begin the process of working out problems yourself.

   Because most executive women are so tight and well controlled at the office, friendships give them a particularly good opportunity to let their hair down. They don't have to be on guard every moment. Candid fantasies, reflections, and memories are among the mutually shared and enjoyed topics in intimate friendships. Friendship adds balance to your life and to your relationship with your significant other—since you can't expect to get everything from your husband or significant other, either. Friends help fill in the gaps and ease the way.

Cultivate your ability to appropriately express a wide range of emotions

SUCCESSFUL FEMALE EXECUTIVES are in touch with their feelings and know when to express them. They don't take their personal life and its problems to work, yet they do find a place to vent them in therapy or with friends. They can experience an array of emotions with varying intensities. They cry when they are sad. They express frustration and disappointment when they are angry. They exude happiness when it's time to celebrate.

Many working women think it is dangerous to be emotionally expressive anywhere—especially in the workplace. But the most successful women in the FESS study were passionate and expressive. Study results indicate that this is not only healthy but also helps reduce stress. Women need to remember that it is possible to be aware of their emotions and still restrict their expression when necessary. They need to carefully choose their places to vent and know when to pull back.

To begin this process, you must first give yourself permission to acknowledge your emotions internally. Then stop after something happens and ask yourself what you are feeling. If you find it difficult to discriminate between emotions, generate a list of common feelings, from despair to euphoria, and carry it with you. It can be enormously helpful to refer to one list if you have time to reflect and are genuinely interested in increasing your sensitivity to your own feelings. When you begin to reveal your emotions to others, choose these people wisely. Don't talk to your secretary or your boss. Experiment with your friends, or if this is a particularly difficult area for you, seek out a therapist to help you learn to talk about how you feel and to be more expressive at the appropriate times.

Broaden your personality to include both "female" and "male" characteristics

TO WORK IN THE PATRIARCHY, women often feel that they must conform to what is thought of as the "male" format for communication processing and expression. Most of my female executive clients do this. Women in business work hard to become more logical, more analytical, more linear in their thinking. This is unfortunate, because they close off another part of themselves in the process that can be very useful in business. In therapy, I guide such women to reenergize and develop both the male and the female sides of themselves.

Women in business work hard to become more logical, more analytical, more linear in their thinking. This is unfortunate, because they close off another part of themselves in the process that can be very useful in business.

While women in the workplace may feel they have to perform a certain role that is narrow and rigid and so-called masculine, and at the same time suppress their feminine side, the FESS study has shown that the women who are the most successful are those who embrace the feminine side and the masculine side simultaneously. They integrate their femininity into their day-to-day lives—professional and personal. They don't shut it off. Instead, they have access to the best of both worlds, a rich and varied repertoire. They adapt well to a variety of situations. They do not don a mask to play a role—they have an internal reference, self-confidence, and self-esteem.

Women who cope successfully are centered. They are comfortable with themselves and are not trying to be something they are not. They can be both compassionate—at one end of the spectrum—or a fiery adversary, whichever reaction is most appropriate to the situation.

In contrast, FESS patients often will doubt their first impressions and their feelings about people, because they have tried so hard and so long to reject what they feel about situations. In sessions, I take notes about their first impressions. Later I remind them of how they felt initially when indeed what they felt is borne out. It is so empowering when they no longer discard what they feel, when they truly learn to validate the emotional side of themselves. They don't lose their edge, as they have feared, but instead hone and sharpen it to a greater definition. They have combined their feminine and masculine sides into something that is truly powerful. With the full benefit of both sides of themselves, their careers take off. As the saying goes, "the whole is greater than the sum of the parts."

This integration of male and female sides refines and focuses the executive woman's understanding of human nature, business, politics, and interpersonal nuances. Having access to her own assertiveness while maintaining a steady hand on her sensitivity and empathy only polishes her corporate skills and transforms her into the ultimate manager.

Exercise vigorously on a regular basis

THIS IS NOT A NEW FINDING by any stretch, however, it is one more reminder that regular and vigorous physical activity is a strong combatant against stress. The most successful women in the FESS study were much more active than were the other more stressed women in the study. Executive women need to make time for exercise several times a week.

In addition to the obvious physical health benefits, there is something tremendously psychologically empowering about defining yourself physically. You learn the perimeters of your physical space, which can be psychologically uplifting. You stand more powerfully on the ground. It is a different kind of strength that adds to your overall power.

It also helps dispel the powerlessness that many of us feel as women when we read, hear, or experience the violence against women in our society. We know that as women—and especially as women who work and travel and who often are burning the midnight oil at the office—we are vulnerable to assault. Having your own physical perimeter defined and rein-forced increases your own sense of potency, effectiveness, mastery, and strength. This helps you send a physical message that can be very effective in your self-protection.

Avoid self-blaming

THE MOST SUCCESSFUL female executives avoid blaming themselves for the problems around them, while the less suc-cessful women have a less healthy tendency to resonate to the hostility and chaos around them. The latter women have pro-grammed themselves to assume that if something goes wrong, it must be their fault. Ironically, there is an underlying grandiosity to the assumption that they are important enough that they should be able to control or fix everything around them. This is a routine distortion of reality that leads them to be too hard on themselves. Instead of thinking about how they might be solving the problem, they expend energy telling themselves they have failed again. What a waste of time and energy.

The women who function best don't feel that way. They accept responsibility when it is due, but do not automatically assume that they are the ones to blame. They don't wallow in the problem; they seek solutions. By automatically focusing on conflict resolution, they get out of their own way. In testing, these women were more often drawn to certain kinds of reactions to problems. Our successful women endorsed behaviors that were diplomatic, deliberate, and well considered.

When a crisis occurred at work, the successful women didn't shoot from the hip or try to elicit an immediate response—bad or good. Many of us, when stressed or feeling vulnerable, tend to release the tension impulsively, to speak before we think. Such candor is only temporarily relieving. The most successful women are more discerning. They are measured. They know when and how to be expressive in a cunning and self-controlled way. Their self-confidence comes with seasoning, and with avoiding the tendency to be too hard on themselves when something goes wrong.

Nurture and guard your self-esteem

IT IS VERY IMPORTANT for executive women to develop and consult their own internal reference. The most successful women trust their own judgment and perception of reality

F
E
S
S

first and foremost, which is a consistent and important way to both nurture and guard their self-esteem. They don't internalize the stress around them, but maintain a cohesive sense of themselves despite outward disruptions. They constantly audit the input they get from other people with self-confidence. When they get feedback from others, they take it as one person's opinion, but do not automatically buy into it. The sound judgment of their own central self makes the final decision.

Even the healthiest people have a tendency to distort reality at times. You should weigh what anyone says to you by deciding if what they are saying is more a function of what they need and how they feel or what is actually happening. Try to interpret the motivation behind the words.

I tell my FESS patients to allow themselves to experiment, go through trial and error, learn from their mistakes. You cannot be successful if you have unrealistic expectations. You are not going to be perfect from day one. If you set yourself up for the impossible, you won't feel good about yourself. Instead, figure out people and situations the best you can. If you temporarily crash and burn, that's okay. View it all as a learning process.

Another important step in nurturing and guarding your self-esteem is carefully choosing the people who will surround you. Choose the people who work for you carefully. Form a good team. Value yourself enough to surround yourself with the best.

To do this, you have to sharpen your insight. It is so common to only see and focus on brief and immediate snapshots of people and situations. Instead, step back and fit these brief snapshots into the overall picture. Again, you have to have faith and trust in your own judgment and ability to do this well. You have to pay attention and track people and situations, and be aware of hidden agendas. Does what you hear fit reality as you perceive it? If not, what other possible agenda is there that does sensibly explain what you see and hear?

Self-esteem also requires patting yourself on the back, something FESS women don't do well. They disregard their own talents and accomplishments. You *have* to nurture yourself, *tell* yourself that you have done a good job. If your performance has fallen short of your expectations, remind yourself that you did your best and that your effort is what really matters. "Positive self-talk" may sound trivial, but it is a huge promoter of self-esteem.

Another important step in nurturing and guarding your self-esteem is carefully choosing the people who will surround you. Choose the people who work for you carefully. Form a good team. Value yourself enough to surround yourself with the best.

Pursue a strong commitment to your profession or your company

JOB INVOLVEMENT was another area that distinguished the healthiest executives from those who were struggling. The healthiest women were in a job where they felt good about what they were doing and where they were doing it.

They were invested in their companies emotionally. That didn't mean everything was perfect on the job, but rather that they cared about what was happening. They felt a part of the successes and failures. They were contributing to a common goal with co-workers. All of these feelings became another important buffer against stress.

You need to identify a path to a meaningful and fulfilling career with your present employer and pursue it to the best of your ability. Be patient, recognizing and accepting that earning your way to the top may be tougher for you than for your male peers. If you feel you're hitting the glass ceiling, quietly investigate to see if you can find evidence to support this. If you conclude that you won't be given any more promotions even if you have earned them, then make a change. Securing a job with an unbiased employer would be far healthier than remaining in a discriminatory, dead-end situation over which you have no power.

Minimize an aggressive, confrontive style of problem solving

WHILE THE LESS SUCCESSFUL WOMEN in the FESS study were characterized by an aggressive, confrontive style of problem solving, the more successful women minimized the use of this tactic. To compensate for working in a patriarchy, many women choose an aggressive, pushy approach; however, according to the FESS research, women are more successful when they avoid unnecessary confrontation and use diplomacy.

Women who are in the aggressive and confrontive mode need to decide what their goals are before they act. Is their goal to resolve the situation, or to simply make themselves feel better by blowing off steam? If they really want to resolve the situation, they have to gear their behavior to be productive and effective. Following is a guide to help you resolve conflict.

F
E
S
S

STEPS TO HEALTHY CONFLICT RESOLUTION

1. Determine your specific goal and how to most effectively communicate that goal.
2. Assess the person to whom you are going to deliver the message and determine how best to get them to listen. Consider setting and time of day. Figure out what makes them tick and play to it.
3. Carefully audit your language to influence their reaction.
4. Convey self-sufficiency. Let them know you are in control and unafraid.
5. Make sure you scrutinize everything the other person says or does.
6. Track their reactions and search for a common ground for conflict resolution.

Critics might say this approach is an endorsement of manipulation. I prefer to call it "effective management." As an executive, you have to manage the people around you or they will manage you. Remember, you are not in a work setting to have completely open and all-trusting work "relationships." You are in a work setting to manage the people around you in ways that will result in the most effective performance.

Monitor your tendency to be aggressive and confrontive, to blurt out responses impulsively, and to exhibit yourself. This behavior increases stress not only for yourself but for those around you—and you run the risk of damaging their confidence in you. While confrontation is sometimes necessary in business, there are methods that women can use to make it both more comfortable and more effective, as shown here:

> Natalie has to do it again. There is no avoiding it this time. She always dreads giving feedback to her secretary. Telling someone you supervise that an aspect of their work is less than perfect is tricky. Natalie depends on Debbie, relies on her loyalty in corporate politics. She remembers her father's wisdom: "An executive's success has more to do with the quality of his supporting staff than you would ever dream." Natalie hates to rock the boat, but there is no way around this problem.
>
> Debbie's a great assistant. Good with numbers, talented in helping with the tedious budget reports Natalie's office has to produce. She works long hours without complaint. She's cheerful and cool under pressure, and full of creative suggestions. She clearly takes her job as seriously as Natalie does when the heat is on.
>
> Debbie's one problem is easy for Natalie to identify. She is chronically late to every meeting. Somehow she manages to get "lost" between her desk and the conference room. It's as if Debbie enters a time warp! It sometimes takes her twice as long to get to a meeting as it does everyone else. Natalie has fantasies of dragging her down the hall just to get her in on time.

Natalie doesn't try to hide her irritation at these moments. The conference room door opens quickly as Debbie silently tiptoes to her chair. Everyone feels the tension between the two women. Debbie tries to stay out of Natalie's view, which is insulting to Natalie. "What does she think, that I'm an idiot? I know she's not here. We've been waiting ten minutes for her so we could get started."

When she calms down, Natalie knows that Debbie means well. But she also knows that if she wants Debbie to be on time, she's going to have to approach the subject carefully. She knows that Debbie will handle their confrontation better at the end of the day when she can leave the office immediately. Debbie is so perfectionistic, she takes everything that isn't completely complimentary as an insult. Natalie often is left feeling that she can't win. She will tell her husband later, "It's as if we weren't having the same conversation . . . I don't know what to do."

Natalie has learned a few things since the last time they had this discussion. She knows to time the meeting to allow Debbie to withdraw, without excuses, to save face. She thinks that listing the excellent performance points first will relax Debbie and help her hear the improvement suggestions better. Natalie knows she will have to watch Debbie closely to clarify any misunderstandings, not letting the negatives cloud the picture. If she really wants a change to occur, she'll have to "pitch it so that Debbie can catch it." She'll have to understand how Debbie views things, as she presents her own perspective. After all, the goal is to negotiate a better way of working together. And Natalie means to succeed.

Embrace a calculated, measured style of problem solving

THE MOST SUCCESSFUL executives are like quicksilver—they are versatile, always changing shapes, adapting to any given situation with speed and efficiency. They change their problem-solving strategies to fit the circumstances. Flexibility is their hallmark. They are constantly adapting to changing environments. They avoid black-and-white thinking and "proven" formulas. They don't expect others around them to conform to their work styles, but rather modify their management style to best fit each employee and each client.

They are able to do this because they have a full range of male-female tactics in their repertoire. They practice "thinking like a man" while not discarding their feminine feelings, and this enables them to deliver a double punch. One very savvy and successful executive woman described it to me as the ability to never lose sight of the greater goal. She was willing to take a short-term hit in exchange for the eventual outcome that she wanted. She remained aware of the big picture at all times.

Women who do not naturally have this characteristic need to rein themselves in from a more explosive or impulsive coping style. Being excessively confrontational does *not* mean you are more powerful. Some of the most powerful people I have known have been quiet and thoughtful—and carefully measured in their statements and actions. When they are moved to action, they are swift, deliberate, and incredibly effective.

If you have feedback from others that you are a poor manager, that you are too blunt or too evasive, you need to first consider the source. Are these people uncomfortable with your power, or is there something in your management style that needs to be softened? Watch carefully how people receive what you are saying. Don't just listen to what you say to them, but scrutinize their reaction. Don't fall prey to the tempting impulse to hear yourself explode as a release. Nothing is accomplished; stress is not reduced by letting off steam in an unproductive way.

Psychologists are taught to listen to the patients' responses carefully. What we say is just an instrument to facilitate a desired effect. The most successful executives bring these psychologist's tools to work.

Take an action-oriented approach to life

THE FIRST NINE of these coping strategies add up to this final and most important step—taking an action-oriented approach to life. This ability flows from possessing a clarity of self, being unambivalent and unapologetic about yourself, and undertaking a full embrace of life. I see that clearly in an executive woman in her mid-forties who has decided to go back and recapture her ballet skills. I see it in women who change careers or start their own businesses. I see it in women who decide to have families after many would say it is too late. I see it in women whose lives look to observers like a fish going rapidly through the water, seamless and with the desired end in sight. These women get what they want in life because they take action and they follow through—in business and personal arenas.

Many of my FESS patients feel paralyzed by life. They feel overwhelmed by their problems and believe that they are helpless to make the necessary changes. Because they are hurting, they have trouble getting out of their own way and seeking effective solutions. Lost in their pain, they sit and throb.

I ask FESS women to reflect on their problems and the effect these situations have on their feelings about themselves. Then I begin to help them work each one out by encouraging them to decide what they can and what they can't do about it. As time goes by, I help them recognize the unhealthy patterns in their lives and how these patterns lead them to do damage to themselves. When they begin to see and understand those patterns themselves, they gradually stop resorting to unhealthy behaviors and distorted thinking. They rely upon their own ego strength to find the way to get them there. Once they believe in themselves, there is no holding them back.

The process of self-activation, of taking charge and living life to the fullest, is a by-product of self-esteem. When you feel better about yourself and you act on your own behalf, you do live life at a higher, more productive level.

I believe that everyone can achieve this state of being. Even if you have suffered a lot of pain in your life, you can learn these skills. They are not innate. You are not born this way. If you have not grown up in a family situation that has shaped and nourished you in this way, you can provide that nourishment for yourself in your adult life. We can all be like the executive women who scored so well on the various questionnaires of the FESS study. Women from every background can achieve this. If you are determined, you can choose the action-oriented approach to life and embrace life as they do. The pain felt by the woman in the following vignette is characteristic of the emotions that paralyze many FESS women and keep them from taking appropriate problem-solving actions:

> The telephone rings and Monica turns over, hoping Ted will pick it up. It's hard to keep up with all his trips. He's in Chicago tonight, the fifth trip there in three weeks. Turning on the light, she picks up the phone, hoping it won't be another hang-up call. Only a dial tone. Again. Ted promised there would be no more women. God! She wants to believe him. She hates to see six years go down the drain.
>
> She met Ted when they were students at Michigan State. He was tall, athletic, at school on a tennis scholarship. A big flirt, he was always surrounded by girls. He had an incredible ability to look deep into a girl's eyes and give her the impression of his full attention. It was a talent he was well aware he had perfected.
>
> His girlfriend before Monica looked like a stand-in for Cindy Crawford. She was gorgeous. Monica was speechless when Ted asked her out. Flustered, every

physical imperfection she had was on the tip of her tongue. She felt hideous. She wanted to blurt out, "Why do you want me?" Ted could see she was tongue-tied. He put his arm around her, saying, "Monica, it's a date, not a proposal. Just nod if you want to go." Monica's body tingled. She was in love.

They've come a long way since that night, getting through business school together and managing to find jobs in the same geographic area. They both excel on the job. Monica is known for her meticulous, well-crafted projects. Management has promoted her many times.

Ted has done equally well. He plays the old boy network like a well-tuned violin. A charming man who could sell ice cream to an Eskimo. Clients' wives love him. He's ambitious, but knows he can go only so far on charm. Not to worry. He always delivers.

His affair came as quite a jolt. Monica's hands still grow cold when she remembers that phone call in March from Ted's lover. "Monica, this is Samantha Jones. I work with your husband. I think we need to talk."

Monica turns over in the empty bed. "We have everything . . . why can't Ted be faithful?" Monica doesn't quite believe that Ted is over Samantha. A slender brunette with "legs that go to heaven." Samantha is every wife's worst nightmare. She is cordial to Monica, but only because she knows she has the upper hand. Monica becomes nauseous with the memory.

Monica has always thought of herself as strong and a "doer." Still shocked by Ted's infidelity, she is even more amazed that she stayed in the marriage. Deep down, she knows those phone calls are from Samantha. She knows that Ted can't stay away from her, and that the affair is ongoing.

Monica gets out of bed and studies her face in the mirror. She can't live this way. The only way to put this pain and humiliation behind her is to leave Ted and what has become a very destructive relationship. As she tells her best friend later, "It's as if something broke inside of me. Ted's history . . . and good riddance."

Growing from a Young Turk into a Seasoned Executive

THERE ARE SEVERAL FACTORS that suggest some of the Young Turks may indeed be younger versions of the Seasoned Executives. They are on average almost five years younger and have about three-and-a-half years less seniority with their present companies than the Seasoned Executives. Yet, they average almost three years more seniority than the Stressed Group though they are two-and-a-half years younger. Also consider that the Young Turks earn far more income than the Stressed Group, and are not far behind the Seasoned Executives—50 percent of them make more than $75,000 a year—yet they are the youngest group in the sample. The Young Turks and the Seasoned Executives clearly have a great deal in common. When you combine those two groups, they are worlds different from the Stressed Group. Some of the Young Turks are headstrong and overly aggressive, but they are smart, and life may teach them that this confrontational, aggressive style frequently doesn't get them what they want. They are too goal oriented and single minded in their thinking, not in an attempt to hurt other people but in an attempt to get to the bottom line quickly and successfully. With any luck, their maturing personalities will be tempered by wisdom, and they will learn to incorporate their softer sides into their behavior and coping styles as newly instated members of the Seasoned Executives. They are young, hard driving, and have been successful, so it seems natural to think that some of them, especially those still in their early thirties, will evolve to an even more adaptive and well-rounded level of maturation. And as they mellow, they will become even more successful.

The Young Turks need to learn that power is gained by letting go of the single-minded, goal-directed approach. Letting go doesn't mean becoming any less organized, prompt, or efficient. It means making room for intuition, feelings, and understanding people. It means being your own good psychologist. When you develop these capabilities, your career abilities will flourish. You will be able to utilize your inborn gifts and talents more effectively. If you are more empathic and have a greater understanding of people, you will read the interpersonal cues and exercise diplomacy—and get what you want. Understanding the psychology of your adversary or business partner is as important as being clear about your own goals and strategies. You must be shrewd. If you go in as the Young Turk with your linear thinking and a "this is the way it has to be done" approach, you are less likely to accomplish your goals. Having that kind of tunnel vision in your life can, over time, inhibit your business judgment and become self-defeating. Your internal psychological constriction can compromise your efforts and limit your achievements.

The Young Turks may be afraid to let go because they have been positively reinforced in both compensation and advancement for being just as they are—driven and linear. But to avoid burnout, to garner greater success, and most importantly, to get to the next step of development, they need to evolve. This evolution results in deals coming together, better use of language, more diplomacy, and less guilt over taking a painful or unpopular stance. And when they disappoint someone, they don't blame themselves. They hit situations head-on in a compassionate way but don't apologize for doing their job. As one woman put it, "I finally became myself."

Mentoring is the way

TO SUPPORT AND PROMOTE optimal evolution in the Young Turks, the Seasoned Executives need to step in and help. Through their mentoring, they can help ensure that Young Turks don't just become Old Turks. This is also how the Seasoned Executive can continue to grow and develop in the last phase of her own career. The best thing a successful female executive can do, for other women and for herself, is to set a positive and guiding example. If she is managing successfully and passing along those skills to others in her office, it will result in a healthier and more effective overall office

F
E
S
S

environment. The Seasoned Executive needs to discourage the "dog-eat-dog" mentality that thrived in the eighties. One of the important, self-actualizing stages in life which further promotes personal and spiritual development is the accepting, compassionate, and encouraging mentoring of someone younger. This is one of the most profound avenues for self-fulfillment. The satisfaction of bequeathing hard-won wisdom and power does result in spiritual peace and well-being. From a broader perspective, if the Seasoned Executive truly believes in equality for the sexes, there is no better way to support and advance this cause than to guide and nurture younger career women through the impassioned pursuit of mentoring opportunities.

> One of the important, self-actualizing stages in life which further promotes personal and spiritual development is the accepting, compassionate, and encouraging mentoring of someone younger. This is one of the most profound avenues for self-fulfillment.

The age spread in our sample between the youngest member of the Young Turks and the oldest member of the Seasoned Executives was a full twenty years. Certain sociological influences may have resulted in their different ways of thinking. While 58 percent of the Seasoned Executives had both their "soft" and "hard" sides fully functioning, only 13 percent of the Young Turks achieved this adaptive balance. One way of understanding this pronounced discrepancy is to look at the sociological influences in the fifties and early sixties. This pre-women's-liberation cultural environment allowed most of the Seasoned Executives to hold on to a positive image of feminine characteristics that either reemerged or stayed with them as they matured. In contrast, the Young Turks were more influenced by the militancy of the seventies and rejected anything that was associated with a traditional feminine side. The Seasoned Executives were exposed to more positive and socially approved forms of femininity growing up, while the Young Turks watched a denouncement of femininity during the bra-burning height of feminism in the seventies.

As a result, the Young Turks may not have a mature and well-rounded appreciation of the highly valuable aspects of femininity. They may fail to differentiate between a healthy, proactive, self-supportive female stance and a pathological, passive, self-sabotaging female stance. In fact, they may view femininity as a weakness. They are, in a sense, a casualty of the radical swing of the feminist movement.

The more feminine sides of their personalities have been undernourished and undeveloped. They may need a positive and caring mentoring relationship with an older woman who enjoys and celebrates her femininity instead of locking it up and hiding it away. Pink does belong in the boardroom, and it looks best on the woman who chairs the meeting.

The Young Turk, as she grows into the Seasoned Executive, may become an even more fully developed and powerful hybrid of her mentor. It is tremendously inspiring for the Young Turks to see a successful woman in front of them showing the way for females to rise to the top. Most of the Seasoned Executives had only male mentors; these men showed them how to become fully developed executives but could not show them how to become fully developed women. Female executive mentoring should be far more enriching

F
E
S
S

and effective for the Young Turks, since their mentors truly understand what it is like to be a woman in a man's world. They lived it themselves. The Seasoned Executives are trailblazing pioneers who have gone into uncharted territory to stake a frontier claim for women. Now they can point to the career path they cleared which is specifically tailored and ideally suited for women. A female mentor can offer another woman a much richer, more well-rounded and comprehensive mentoring experience because she will connect on all levels—not just how to be a better executive, but being a woman in business, a wife, a mother. These mentors are providing a woman-to-woman gift to their charges that their own male mentors were unable to give them.

The power bestowed by the Seasoned Executive on the Young Turk also may be more lasting in nature. When her male mentor retired, the Seasoned Executive often was left without true power; her power fell under the man's umbrella of influence and was lost when the mentor left. This is a danger inherent in having a male mentor. The Young Turk mentored by the Seasoned Executive should be able to find a more durable, lasting, and stable place of authority in her company; her own power is something she can count on. The following example shows how beneficial mentoring can be to an up-and-coming executive:

> Jackie's philosophy is simple. She long ago figured out that the secret to success has to do with casting out childhood fantasies about people. Simply put, not everyone is your friend. Most people will use you in a

New York minute if that's what they need. The conse-quences to you are immaterial.

As a girl, she wanted everyone to like her, even if she paid a high price for their regard. Terribly hurt when her best friend sold her out for her own silly agenda in high school, Jackie vowed never to let something like that happen to her again. She no longer lets herself trust easily. Early on, in every rela-tionship, she figures out what a person's true agenda is. And Jackie is not easily fooled. People respect her for that.

Jackie is an able strategist. Incredibly bright, she focuses on situations with a unique intensity, discard-ing nonessentials, selecting only those facts that are most important. Her enemies quip that she is like a Velociraptor from Jurassic Park. Moving with stealth, she'll outwit her opponent with rapier-like precision. It's actually fun to watch—if you're on her team.

No one underestimates her more than once. Petite, blonde, and toned, Jackie favors achromatic suits with lean lines. The better my silhouette, she thinks, the more seriously I'll be taken. None of those bright colors and shorter skirts for Jackie. Looking feminine in the office compromises her credibility—or so she thinks.

Jackie's rise in the company has been meteoric. Though barely thirty years old, she commands a six-figure salary. Tough problems are her specialty. Since deal making is a large part of her job, she knows that hard work is not enough. She is a master in the art of negotiation, knowing how to keep her mouth shut when she needs to, but demanding what she wants whenever necessary.

While Jackie can size up her competition in microseconds, she is completely unable to massage the egos of corporate clients. "Jackie, you've got to learn patience," her mentor Suzanne repeatedly tells her. "I know you're right and you know you're right. But the customer holds the chips, and you don't get in their face about it." Another reprimand, but one she knows she deserves.

Suzanne is respected by all of her employees. As the number two person in purchasing, she combines a high company profile with a gracious attitude. But back her against a wall and she's as tough as nails. If you burn her once, she'll make sure it's only once. The consequences for crossing her are stiff. One woman was transferred overseas when she went after Suzanne's job. She never knew what hit her.

Suzanne likes Jackie; she identifies with her. She sees her as a younger version of herself. Jackie's drive, perseverance, and single-mindedness are all familiar qualities. She knows that Jackie's impatience and lack of diplomacy, however, are liabilities. If she can smooth those rough edges, she might have a winner. Jackie has the right idea, but she needs to mellow, to become more discriminating in picking her battles. She needs to learn it isn't necessary to win every battle to win the war.

Suzanne's time is scarce, and allocating energy to Jackie's tutelage is a huge investment. But she's watched Jackie handle herself for a number of years now and she has a thorough understanding of her strengths and weaknesses. Suzanne hates to see Jackie make pivotal political mistakes at this point in her young career. She wants to shield her from key blunders. Jackie needs to learn to listen, to exercise control and deliberation in decision making, and to remember that client opinion can make or break your climb up the ladder. Jackie will make it, but only if she learns these lessons. Suzanne plans to give her an edge by making sure that she does.

CHAPTER 8

FESS and the American Society: A Prescription for Change

*W*ITH THE CAUSES AND EFFECTS of FESS fully explained, there still remains the question—how can FESS be prevented on a large scale? I am convinced that without a rejuvenation of the feminist movement—recreated in a form that appeals to a broad spectrum of women—we will not have the widespread societal change needed to prevent FESS.

The feminist movement is now plagued by a bimodal distribution of philosophies. At one end of the spectrum are the radical feminists, and on the other, the antifeminists. There are very few believers in the middle. Those of us who find ourselves there—as I do—can fully expect to be shot at from both sides. Yet I believe that it is this central position that will eventually attract enough women to form the new-and-improved next wave of feminism.

F
E
S
S

I argue for a feminist movement that is realistic and functional. This type of feminist enjoys being feminine and flirtatious and alluring to her partner while being nurturing to her family and friends. She wears her pearls, pink, and sculptured nails to the boardroom if it suits her. She is passionate about her children and unapologetically protective of their futures. She wants her daughters to succeed as well as her sons.

The feminist's professional self is just another reflection of the powerful, fully developed woman she has let herself become. Unencumbered, she rises to each occasion in her personal and business life with strength, class, and compassion. She chooses the best solution to each situation, but refuses to sacrifice herself to earn approval. She'll agree to disagree in conflict resolution, but demand respect above all else.

> I argue for a feminist movement that is realistic and functional.
> This type of feminist...wears her pearls, pink, and sculptured nails to the boardroom if it suits her.

This type of feminist enjoys being a woman and having the power she has earned. She is committed to the feminist movement and the hope and promise it holds for our society. She regards equal pay for equal work as a given. She remains politically aware and socially concerned. She is psychologically nurturing to herself, her partner, and her friends. She believes equality is vital in all relationships, whether business or personal.

Psychologically, what has happened to the feminist movement can be compared to what happened with McCarthyism in the fifties. There is an artificial division of feelings toward people into all good and all bad. The movement is characterized by extremely rigid black-and-white thinking. Both sides have a very concrete way of looking at the world. You have intelligent, successful women who are antifeminists running around saying feminists are crazy, that women can relax, all men are wonderful, and equality is here. Then you have the radical feminists who hate every man and those women who cavort with men. Neither extreme position is grounded in reality. Equality is not here—women still do not earn equal pay for equal work; women are still hitting a glass ceiling in corporate America; women still shoulder an unequal burden of household and child-rearing responsibilities. On the other hand, men are not all evil, violent beast masters determined to hold women back from achievement.

While many liberal feminists believe that a widespread conspiracy exists to keep women in their place, it is not a conspiracy but ingrained sociological beliefs that continue to cause problems for women in America. As women progress, as we push the glass ceiling upward, we continue to collide with values and beliefs that are centuries old. People—men, women, black, white, yellow, red, and brown—are threatened when others challenge their beliefs about how the world works. Women trying to rise through the corporate ranks is foreign and threatening to many men and other women, and it provokes a negative visceral reaction. These men—and even women—don't conspire, but naturally react to such change in both overt and subtle ways.

A prescription for positive change

THE GOOD NEWS is that women have made huge strides and continue to progress. Change comes slowly in all things. Following is a prescription for positive changes—some are societal, others are personal. They all can further the advancement toward equality.

Let go of stereotypes

In spite of herself, Cynthia is feeling nervous again. It's time for her to go to work. Her husband, Will, holds their nine-month-old daughter in his arms and tells Cynthia to have a good day at the office.

Fate played a cruel trick on them when Will was abruptly laid off from the company he had been with for seven years. Neither of them saw it coming. Cynthia had been on maternity leave from her company at the time, but they were happy to welcome her back early and place her on full salary.

She hates to leave her baby. She feels sick when she thinks about it. She makes a good salary, and her family can get by on her earnings for quite some time if need be. After four months, Will's job hunting hasn't turned up any promising prospects. Will tries to be upbeat, but Cynthia knows the situation is hard on them.

Ironically, Will is having an easier time than Cynthia coping with this role reversal. He good-naturedly assumes all of the child care and household responsibilities, and he does a good job running the home and caring for their daughter. At parties, he jokes about being a "real-life Mr. Mom," and he even greeted Cynthia's return home one day in a full-length apron. Cynthia had winced. She didn't find his little joke funny and made him promise never to wear the apron again in her presence.

Sometimes Cynthia cries while she's driving to work. Her tears confuse her. She loves her job and her relationship with Will. She isn't worried about the welfare of her daughter, because Will does as good a "mothering" job as she does. He loves the baby, he loves being a father, and he keeps the house in good shape—even tending their garden.

Cynthia likes being at work once she gets there. But something about the whole arrangement just doesn't feel right! This is not what she signed up for. Cynthia always thought that her own mother was too conservative and old-fashioned, believing that "a woman's place was in the home." In college, she had had endless debates with her parents about feminism and gender roles. Now Cynthia is confronting sexism once again—her own. She tells her best friend, Katie: "I can't believe I'm like this. I always thought stereotypes were stupid. Now I'm seeing how hypocritical I really am."

Katie thinks Cynthia is being too hard on herself; after all, the stress of going from two professional incomes to one would drive anyone crazy. She advises her to reserve judgment until there is more equity in breadwinning. If her bias remains at that point, she should probably do some soul-searching. Until then, she says, "Lighten up on yourself; you're dealing with a lot."

As illustrated above, both men and women need to stop clinging to outdated stereotypes of each other. It is time to raise the consciousness of the workplace, because the existing state of affairs is hurting us all. As was pointed out in chapter 3, studies have shown that both "family-oriented" men and "career-oriented" women are denied rewards in the workplace. We need to transcend the old cultural stereotypes, rigidly programmed in our society, and expend effort to open up opportunities for both women and men to grow in ways that now are seen as "different." It is not a universal truth that women are homemakers and caretakers and men must be the providers. It is only a cultural dictate—a rule that can be broken and changed.

We need to become "gender blind" in the corporate world. So much of the problem is very subtle. When my husband and I were co-directors of the psychology department in a psychiatric hospital, I was treated with as much respect as he was, yet co-workers always called me "Sylvia" and called him "Dr. Gearing." I didn't care. I wasn't insulted. But the subtle difference was there. I didn't feel insulted at the time.

I believe "gender blindness" can be achieved. Already, you can see the difference between generations. The Twenty-something generation grew up for the most part with moms who worked full-time, who commanded more power at home and in the workplace than the mothers of the Fortysomething or Thirtysomething generations. I think over time, as companies continue to work on diversity issues through seminars and workshops, consciousness will be raised and change will occur.

The women interviewed for this book time and again pointed to the older white males as the group most resistant to change. "Some of the older guard do have a very hard time taking directions from a woman," said one. "With people in my own age group, my peers, I don't sense that. I don't feel that at all. The older dinosaurs—that's where the difficulty is." As this World War II generation retires from the workforce, resistance will diminish.

You can hear the hope in the voices of women who have achieved power the hard way: "I think that now as the younger people are coming up, especially the younger males, I think they are truly accepting the situation that women work. I find that their reactions are so much better."

> Change will have to come from a grass roots level and will have to begin with the mass media refusing to adhere to decades-old dictums.

Getting away from stereotypes will be difficult. They are everywhere. There is a lack of critical thinking in American society that is disturbing. Change will have to come from a grass roots level and will have to begin with the mass media refusing to adhere to decades-old dictums.

Take your risks—and rewards

MUCH OF THE POPULAR WISDOM identifies women's resistance to taking risks as a reason for lack of advancement to the highest positions in corporate America. A July 1994 article in *Working Woman*, however, pointed out two recent studies showing that women don't get the promotions men do because they don't get as many opportunities to prove themselves—they don't get the risks or the rewards. While part of the problem may be misguided attempts by male managers to protect women from defeat, as was pointed out in these studies, there is much women can do individually to gain the limelight.

As was pointed out in the book *Members of the Club*, many women executives forget the all-important task of bringing in business. Hardworking and task oriented, they have their noses to the grindstone instead of their eyes open, looking for new deals. Too often, the safe route has worked for them. In high school and college, working harder was enough to keep them at the top of the class. In those venues, hard work and intelligence was enough to keep them ahead of the boys. Yet in business, their male counterparts are willing to risk all for the biggest deal, and surge ahead time after time. Taking risks is an often foreign concept that women must embrace to make it to the top (Driscoll and Goldberg, 1993).

Taking risks and bringing in business to the firm generally requires increased business travel. And in the future, when some of the best opportunities for corporate business will be in the international arena, this will be even more true. Many women feel harnessed by their increased sense of responsibility for home and children, but there is really no reason why they can't succeed in the international arena if they are willing to make the sacrifices.

F
E
S
S

Women who want to succeed in this arena must have their family life in order first. Being organized and responsible enough to hire the right caretaker, making sure the home bases are covered, will give women the confidence to succeed in the business world. There is a price, of course: time spent away from family. But executive women who have found a balance often compensate with extra time off after long business trips.

Additionally, if you must travel to excel, it is vital that you maintain a reasonable work week when you are not traveling. This is the area where tough choices abound. You will not be able to maintain a healthy parenting relationship if you do not put in the time and the energy. If traveling is a must, guard your home time with a vengeance. Children are better able to tolerate a traveling mother if they see you physically and emotionally available at other times. Make sure that your spouse or secondary caretaker is supportive of your situation and of the arrangements you have made for the children while you are away.

> Being organized and responsible enough to hire the right caretaker, making sure the home bases are covered, will give women the confidence to succeed in the business world.

Formalize the old girl network

WOMEN NEED TO FORMALIZE the old girl network and take it seriously to support women in the rise to the top. Again, hard work is not enough. Corporate America is a political game and women need the support of a strong party, a woman's party, behind them.

Supporting the old girl network doesn't mean behaving like men, and it doesn't mean favoring women over men just for the sake of catching up. It does mean embracing a new prototype of woman, one who can be powerful and feminine, who knows how to use feminine sensitivities and intuition, who can show compassion for people but is not a lifeguard out to save all the swimmers, and who is not apologetic about her own power.

We need to redefine ourselves personally as women, professionally as women, and collectively as women along these lines.

Women do defeat themselves by not supporting each other, yet if we *only* support women at the expense of men, we risk everything. If we are biased against men, we risk a backlash that threatens any progress we have made. Treating men the way we were treated will only result in a negative view of networking among women and will undermine our accomplishments. Choosing to only support women results in the same tokenism we have experienced. I don't want affirmative action for women, yet if I find myself in proximity to a very capable woman with a superior product, I will support her. But that support will be given because of her product and service, not because of her gender.

Mentoring is another important step in supporting women and solidifying the old girl network. Mentoring means helping other women understand how you achieved your position, and it means having frank and open discussions with other women

> Women do defeat themselves by not supporting each other, yet if we *only* support women at the expense of men, we risk everything. If we are biased against men, we risk a backlash that threatens any progress we have made.

about the gender bias that exists in corporate America. I worry about the tendency of antifeminists to underestimate the gender bias that still is very strong in our society. Such a perspective is naive and misses the point. Women must be fully aware of all of the rules of the game, including those designed to compromise their power.

Women in business need to actively think about grooming other women for leadership. The trail has been blazed, but we still need to pave the way for other women to take power.

Embrace "Power Feminism"

WOMEN NEED A RALLYING POINT so that there is a common psychological language to strengthen them collectively. The new "Power Feminism" called for by feminist Naomi Wolf could bring together the varying fragments of the feminist movement. This kind of unifying banner is essential to reenergizing the feminist movement and the quest for equality. As Naomi Wolf has written, we need to forget the idea that we are all going to be homogeneous. The next wave of the feminist movement will be a movement of diversity, of all ages, all identities, and all backgrounds. As shown in the following example, intolerance bars the alliance between women that is necessary for power feminism to develop:

> For one of the first times in her life, Candace is speechless. Her quick-witted responses, even to hostile and demeaning male superiors, has marked her rise in the executive ranks of her corporation. Candace

F
E
S
S

generally is tactful and has a deft verbal touch, but all of her business associates know that she is a tough lady who won't let herself be pushed around. A battle-scarred veteran of many corporate wars, Candace is not the least bit intimidated when a young hotshot named Meg joins the company. But Meg has just confronted Candace so effectively that Candace has no rebuttal. She's stunned.

Candace hasn't liked Meg from the beginning. She's too brash, too aggressive, too unfeminine. Meg is a bright and driven workaholic who gets the job done and done well. Candace can't quibble with Meg's results, she just doesn't like her style. Candace enjoys being a wife and mother outside of work, and she reacts negatively to Meg's lack of balance. Too rough, too linear, she mutters to herself after talking to Meg. As a result, Candace doesn't lift a finger to help Meg in any way, and occasionally Candace works the office political scene to subtly undermine Meg. Over time, Candace succeeds and Meg's popularity and "whiz kid" reputation suffer.

One Friday afternoon, as Candace gets ready to leave for the weekend, a male friend walks into the office suite. Candace smiles as she jokes, "It's time for us to leave for the weekend, but girl-wonder Meg can run the company in our absence!" She doesn't notice Meg standing right behind the door. Candace is thunderstruck when Meg rounds the corner and says, "You know, I can't understand why you sabotage me every chance you get. I hoped that you would welcome the chance to help another woman. You've done nothing but try to destroy my work."

Candace flushes bright red, and Meg turns and leaves. Her male friend's tactfully silent exit doesn't help her feel any better. She is astonished to find herself thinking over and over, Meg is right. She has to face her own hidden agendas and she is ashamed. She remembers all the diversity and mentoring workshops she has attended over the last three years. How can she have let herself fall into such a trap? Even if she isn't willing to go all out for Meg, that's no reason to stamp her into the ground. Candace has a lot to think about this weekend.

Much of Naomi Wolf's Power Feminism is about recognizing power within ourselves as women...as little girls, we may boss the entire preschool around the playground. Then as teens, we seem to shrink into the boxes society has built for us.

Undermining other women in the workplace serves no good purpose and ultimately hurts us all. We must tolerate the differences among those women who join the next feminist movement while remaining united on the basic principles. We shouldn't expect to agree with every lifestyle, but we must respect the right of each woman to pursue the lifestyle that works best for her. And we must be realistic in our expectations of the feminist movement. After all, it is not a religion—it is a point of view.

Much of Naomi Wolf's Power Feminism is about recognizing power within ourselves as women. Boys are reared to capture the flag, to grab the power that is theirs. Too often, girls are not encouraged to take charge. As little girls, we may boss the entire preschool around the playground. Then as teens, we seem to shrink into the boxes society has built for us.

Women need to learn to capture the flag. They need to define who they are now and who they want to be in the future. The clearer they are about the parameters of that self and the goals of that self, the more others will conform to their agenda. If you are perfectly clear about who you are and where you want to go, it is far easier to move into a position of power and responsibility and make it your own.

The women interviewed for this book had no problem accepting their power. Their positions of confidence were excellent sources of strength in the political warfare that is a reality in corporate America. So much of corporate interplay is a matter of understanding the weak points of others and exploiting them. Only if you are confident can you play and win. Intuition, listening to yourself and your gut, tracking your initial reactions to people, learning to trust yourself, can help you build confidence over time.

Women who have recovered from FESS, who have learned to incorporate their female selves into their jobs, do find a renewed power. As one says, "I used to spend a lot of time trying to be one of the guys, trying to be tough and always trying to have sort of a left-brain approach to being competent. Now I'm exploring the other strengths that I have. I've demonstrated that I'm good with the left-brain stuff, but I'm exploring what strengths I have as a woman that are inherent to being a woman, or unique to being me, that make me successful. It's gotten to the point where if I don't learn how to be successful as myself, I don't want to be successful on their terms anymore. It costs too much."

Another important aspect of Power Feminism is saying no to guilt—guilt about child care, guilt about commanding power, guilt about saying no to people who waste your time, guilt about delegating tasks that you simply do not have time to do as you take on more responsibility in leadership. As women take themselves more seriously, they naturally let go of the guilt that can be debilitating. Your time is a resource, and you need to guard it well.

The executives I have worked with have been good models for me. I have learned how to manage my time better and let go of guilt. As seniority increases, your responsibilities increase. In my own life, I found myself repeatedly getting into a position where I couldn't do everything. I had to delegate, and I had to be sure that I was taken seriously in delegating tasks, because the results were always a reflection on me. But the first step in assuming power in the workplace was legitimizing power within myself. Before I took that step, I was constantly second-guessing myself.

The next step in Power Feminism is acknowledging our own achievements. I still struggle with that personally, and with the visibility that comes with success. Even though I often have found myself in the position of knowing what I am talking about and knowing more than anyone else, as a woman, I was conditioned to hold the view of myself as dependent on others for information. When you live Power Feminism, you reference yourself. You become your own resource. You recognize your own expertise along with that of others.

Another important step is recognizing leadership abilities in women. When your daughter or son asks, "Have there been any women presidents, Mom?" reply, "Not officially, dear, but we're working on it." Make sure you communicate to the next generation the right to leadership and power for both sexes. Women need to acknowledge and celebrate the gifts and abilities of the women around them. The support we give to women today may enable the emergence of revolutionary female leadership that will change the world for the better.

Stop sabotaging other women

WOMEN SABOTAGING OTHER WOMEN is just as damaging to the move toward equality as the discrimination that is innate in patriarchal society. I have conducted many interviews that make it plain woman-on-woman sabotage is alive and well in corporate America. Women in subordinate positions often sabotage women in power, and women in power keep those attempting to rise from advancing because they want to remain queen bee.

Women need to become gender-centric. While avoiding discrimination against men, we at least need to prevent women from hurting women. Women need to stick together, because many men are not going to help us fight for equality. It is imperative we change our mind-set and stop competing with women so fiercely.

I was reared in a time when women didn't aid other women: they were all adversaries in the competition for men. Instead of repeating this old mistake, we have to redefine ourselves as people. We can be far better than adversaries on a sexual battlefield. We need to learn to prize and celebrate the achievements of women as a group. This will lead to changes in the perceptions and stereotypes of all of us. We need to realize that one of the biggest weapons against sexism is supporting each other.

Don't underestimate your foe: sexism

MOST OF THE EXECUTIVES INTERVIEWED for this book were not currently experiencing sexual harassment. However, almost everyone interviewed had experiences with harassment earlier in their careers. When they were in their twenties and thirties, when they had no power and were in subordinate or training positions, they were vulnerable. Their vulnerability was a combination of youth, their lack of power, and a general naïveté. Basically, many of them found themselves in compromising positions and did not know how to get out.

As they increased in seniority and came into their own authority, the experiences with harassment decreased. Humor became their most potent weapon in the sex games at work. With humor, they learned to contain sexual harassment before they were in a compromising position.

When humor doesn't work to stop harassment, a direct approach often does. Every woman needs to be clear and frank about her limits and when the harasser has stepped across the line. Get in his face if a frank airing of the problem doesn't work. Bring in a witness to the conversation if he doesn't take you seriously. Take yourself seriously, and eventually he will have no other choice.

Corporations need to have workshops and seminars to educate the entire workforce about harassment and to provide a clear structure for appropriate behavior. Corporations must not underestimate the psychological damage that can be caused by sexual harassment. It can be very damaging to self-esteem, and if it is constant, it can contribute to sleeplessness, eating disorders, and many other physical health problems associated with extreme stress. Harassment keeps women from advancing to more powerful positions because it functions as the cat's paw for the old status quo. Harassment is not only damaging to women, but to business as a whole. It stifles creativity and freedom. And it negatively affects the productivity of both victims and perpetrators.

Sexual discrimination also is damaging to business, since it often means that ideas from the female half of the workforce are not taken seriously. While many of the executives in this book did not express concern about sexual harassment in their present positions, they were, without exception, extremely frustrated by sexual discrimination.

While I don't want to stereotype all men as being sexist, since increasing numbers of men are very open to the advancement and contributions of women in business, women should not kid themselves. Don't underestimate the amount of sexism you are facing from the old guard. You must play hardball and stay on your toes. Many women would like to think that we are all friends working toward a common goal. They are open and trusting and friendly—all excellent qualities. But when the water is full of sharks, you must guard against being bitten. And remember, the further along you get on the ladder, the more subtle the discrimination.

Listen to the frustration of some top level executives:

"I would make a suggestion on how to approach a problem and they would slough it off. Then later on, they would come back to the exact thing I'd said . . ."

"They're always looking for some source to confirm what I've said. It really makes me crazy. They'll always ask, 'And what do you think, Lisa?' Then they'll say, 'Does anybody here agree with what she says?' My direct supervisor is probably the biggest chauvinist I have met. Sometimes he's subtle, but sometimes he'll even say things like 'You know the role of a woman is in the home.' "

Get political

WOMEN EXECUTIVES WORK HARD—sometimes too hard for their own good. You must allow time and breathing room to pay attention to the political game.

Part of being an executive is participating in the many extracurricular activities expected of you. It is in these meetings and on these committees where much of the politics of a company is seen and heard. Being a woman, and probably one of few women at a higher level, the extra demands are even greater. As one executive put it, "This is an additional burden that women executives are bearing that nobody is really thinking about."

The authors of *Members of the Club* recognize this point. Often politics is about quality, not quantity. Choose your positions wisely. Jockey for a seat on the key committee, not just any committee. Look for the committees that give you an opportunity to show your best stuff so that you can demonstrate your abilities. If it's not happening, move on.

Many female executives are the only ones of their gender at the top, and are therefore asked to sit on every committee that comes along. Set your own limits on how many extracurricular committees you are willing to join. Once you are a committee member, scope out and recognize the agenda at hand, and consider discussing openly with the rest of the committee that you know you are there, in part, because you are a woman. With that out in the open, the rest of the committee is more likely to take you and your input seriously.

> Cultivate your protégés and use them to spread your own influence wider by appointing them to sit in on meetings you cannot attend. As you climb the corporate ladder, protect your protégés and adopt the attitude of "Don't touch my lady" to build trust.

Mentoring is another part of the political game. Cultivate your protégés and use them to spread your own influence wider by appointing them to sit in on meetings you cannot attend. As you climb the corporate ladder, protect your protégés and adopt the attitude of "Don't touch my lady" to build trust.

The characteristics that psychologically enable you to achieve an executive position in an antifemale atmosphere are crucial in the political game. Playing your cards close to your chest, being very politically wary—not to a point of distrust, but employing a healthy cynicism—are all essential. You cannot succeed taking things at face value. You must try to see and understand hidden agendas. These tactics are universal, and women cannot afford to ignore them. Women have to be careful and skillful at sidestepping bombs that are cast in their way.

The authors of *Members of the Club* erroneously underestimate the power of the glass ceiling. They say that "focusing on the existence of a glass ceiling keeps many women powerless." They seem to believe that the glass ceiling is nothing more than a cop-out for women who don't succeed. This viewpoint denies the reality of sexual discrimination today. While progress has been made, we are far from where we need to be. Women are still being sabotaged by men and need to be alert to their maneuvers. Countless highly successful female executives deliver the bottom line, but there is *still* an unequal system in American business that favors men. Period.

When you reach the very top, however, the executive women interviewed say the politics change. You have the power. You are part of the inner circle, and your power can soften the gender barrier that has kept you watching your back for years. There is nothing you have to prove to those who are on the rise. After your steep climb, you can begin to catch your breath and establish a new equilibrium. At this high place, you can let go of some of that old self-protection and cynicism as you establish a new psychological discourse that is more open. At the very top, you can give and receive information more freely. Once there, mentoring is again useful as a way to help you stay aware of corporate intricacies through people in junior positions whom you trust and who trust you.

If you don't reach this trusting place, or if you see that you are not making headway in company politics, know when to quit. Sometimes you have to be willing to accept defeat, because there are some systems that are impenetrable where you cannot win. You must be willing to move on to an environment that is healthier and more conducive to your progress.

Get flexible

FLEXIBILITY is both a personal and societal mandate. For corporate America to be successful in the future, as the many different alternative lifestyles become the norm and the fifties' notions of home, work, and family become nearly nonexistent, we must all be more flexible and open to new views of the way the world works.

Our society needs to give more moral support to working parents—men and women. We need to acknowledge that there should be and must be a dual role, and place a higher value on rearing children.

Child care is a major issue for us all, not just for mothers who work. The best antidote to the guilt that goes with leaving children at home or in day care is to practice one of the most basic principles of successful child care. As a family therapist, I have treated many unhappy families. One of the first concepts I try to instill in them is that to be able to parent successfully, you must be in a good place yourself as a person. That leaves a lot of choices for parents. If you are

most fulfilled staying home and that works with your marriage and educational background, that's fine. If you need to
get back to work full-time to feel fulfilled, your child will
only benefit from that.

Your child takes cues for his or her own well-being from
you. You must find the correct balance for your family. If you
are dropping your children off at 6:00 A.M. and are gruff and
angry and hurried, and you pick them up at 6:00 P.M. in the
same horrible mood, obviously you need to find a better way.
But I see executive women every day whose kids are in day
care, who are happy with themselves, and who have successful
children. In my practice, the kids I've seen who are the most
unhappy are those whose parents are going through an angry
divorce. The second most troubled group seems to be those
children with mothers who stay at home full-time and exploit
their children to meet their own psychological needs. Those
are some of the toughest cases to treat successfully, because
those mothers will fight you to the death to keep you from
making their kid healthy in a way that separates mother and
child. A distant third is the group of career women who
haven't been able to spend time with their kids. Such a child
feels neglected and lonely. In each case, the child is the symp-
tom bearer of the dysfunction in the parent's life.

Accepting change

THE GOOD NEWS is that managers, male and female, are
beginning to recognize the positive effects of diversity and
flexibility on productivity and creativity in the workforce. As

FESS

managers recognize that these issues affect the bottom line, change should come more easily. Here patience is a virtue, because I am convinced that with another active wave of the feminist movement, our work will be finished and the world will be a better place for both genders.

As a psychologist who has worked with hundreds of clients, I am always deeply impressed by the difficulty people have with change of any kind, good or bad. Feminism that assures the equality of women introduces a profound change that is frightening to people of both sexes. Men may fear a loss of power, status, and role definition. Women may fear a loss of predictability, an increase in demands and responsibilities, and an unwanted independence that makes them feel vulnerable.

Men and women who harbor these viewpoints must recognize them as fear-based and misleading. This is an essential step in accepting change.

A social system that rigidly defines any of us will strangle the next generation and snuff out its potential. The complexity and richness of the human spirit cannot be nurtured and cultivated in a system that seeks to disempower half of our society. Only when men and women fully grasp the significance of this centrally based feminist edict—equality for all people irrespective of gender—will we be able to evolve as a whole society. Without the full participation of women in American

> Only when men and women fully grasp the significance of this centrally based feminist edict—equality for all people irrespective of gender—will we be able to evolve as a whole society. Without the full participation of women in American business, we may be deprived of some of our greatest achievements.

business, we may be deprived of some of our greatest achievements.

A new social order acknowledging gender equality requires the tolerance of ambiguity; none of us knows for sure what may happen. Ambiguity can cause anxiety, which, happily, can often lead to dramatic and positive change. Our culture is in the throes of a massive social shift in attitudes toward women. Part of the time, many of us, including myself, cling to old stereotyped definitions of reality. There is a comfort in what is familiar. We can count on it.

Unfortunately, unless equality in the executive suite is achieved for women, corporate America may find itself unable to compete globally over time. We must infuse fresh perspectives and creativity into business strategies. We have to reach a better appreciation of the potential inherent in a truly diverse workforce. America needs this firepower to compete successfully in the new millennium. "Gender-blended" focus groups may be the new basis for achieving true excellence.

Imagine the power of men and women of all races successfully working for the same goal rather than against one another. Visualize the qualitatively superior end products of male-female teamwork and togetherness. It is within our grasp, if we reach as one.

APPENDIX I

QUESTIONNAIRES EMPLOYED IN THE FESS STUDY

FESS Study Information Sheet:
This brief questionnaire gathered background information about age, education, marital status, and children, and also asked several questions about type of work, employer, and general work environment. In addition, questions were included on leisure time, arrangements with mate about chores and parenting, comparison of the woman's salary with her mate's salary, and sexual harassment experiences. This questionnaire had no formal scales.

Female Executive Stress Syndrome Questionnaire:
This questionnaire was created especially for this study. It contains ten scales that explore the nature and severity of tension-producing environmental demands, such as sexual discrimination, job burnout, social and family relationships, and perceived expectations of perfection. The questionnaire also includes a composite score that represents the average score of the ten scales and serves as a general barometer of overall stress. Higher scores indicate that the stressful situation being examined is more severe in its negative impact upon the individual.

Bem Sex-Role Inventory (Bem, 1981):
This inventory was designed originally to facilitate research on psychological androgyny. The concept of androgyny assumes that an individual can strongly identify with both masculine traits and feminine traits and attain a healthy balance or combination of the two types of sex-role characteristics. The inventory contains a Femininity Scale and a Masculinity Scale that allows the individual to score high on both scales, high on one scale and low on the other (including a strong identification with only one set of sex-role traits), or low on both scales (indicating a lack of identification with both masculine and feminine traits, which is labeled as undifferentiated sex-role identification). Higher scores on either scale indicate a stronger identification with the corresponding sex-role traits.

Coopersmith Self-Esteem Inventory (Coopersmith, 1981):
This brief inventory focuses on self-esteem, which is conceptualized as an individual's relatively stable and enduring attitudes and judgments of her/his self-image. The inventory produces a single score; this acts as a global indicator of high self-esteem versus low self-esteem. Higher scores correspond to higher levels of self-esteem.

Coping Resources Inventory (Hammer and Marting, 1988): This inventory evaluates the presence of several different coping resources that equip an individual to deal effectively with a wide variety of stressful situations while minimizing symptoms caused by such situations and/or minimizing the time required to recover from these situations. Five individual scales examine cognitive, social, emotional, spiritual/philosophical, and physical coping resources. In addition, a total resource estimation is obtained by adding together the five scale scores. As a scale score gets higher, the corresponding coping resource is seen as stronger or more dominant in the individual's personality.

Jenkins Activity Survey (Jenkins, Zyzanski, and Rosenman, 1979):
This survey assesses the presence of the Type A behavior pattern that research has linked with coronary heart disease. One scale investigates the presence of the basic pattern itself, while the other three scales investigate the presence of the three basic components of Type A behavior: speed and impatience characteristics; job involvement characteristics (approximating a workaholic pattern); and hard-driving and competitive characteristics. Higher scores on each scale indicate a more pronounced presence of its characteristics.

Profile of Mood States (McNair, Lorr, and Droppleman, 1992):
This questionnaire produces a profile that describes the relative intensity of different kinds of emotional states. Five of the scales focus on negative, or problematic, emotional states (e.g., anxiety, depression, anger, fatigue, and confusion). A sixth scale focuses on vigor, a positive and desirable emotional state. A Total Mood Disturbance Score is calculated by summing the five problematic mood state scales and then subtracting the vigor scale score from this sum. In general, higher scores on any scale correspond to more severe or extreme symptoms of the emotional state examined.

Ways of Coping Questionnaire (Folkman and Lazarus, 1988):
This questionnaire examines the thoughts and actions of an individual in reaction to a specific stressful situation. Instead of focusing on generalized coping resources that might be applied in several situations, this instrument targets the specific strategies used for *one* stressful situation that was encountered in the past week. The coping strategies involved include confrontive coping, distancing, self-controlling, seeking social support, accepting responsibility, escape-avoidance, planned problem solving, and

positive reappraisal. Higher scores indicate a more pronounced presence of the coping strategy being measured, although the test makers emphasize that they do *not* assume that any of these coping strategies are necessarily adaptive or desirable.

FEMALE EXECUTIVE STRESS SYNDROME QUESTIONNAIRE

Please circle **ONE AND ONLY ONE** number **UNDER** each item in accordance with the following key:

-3	-2	-1	0	+1	+2	+3
Strongly Disagree	**Somewhat Disagree**	**Slightly Disagree**	**No Opinion**	**Slightly Agree**	**Somewhat Agree**	**Strongly Agree**

SEXUAL HARASSMENT SCALE

1. My male co-workers treat me with respect, courtesy, and professionalism.

    -3   -2   -1   0   +1   +2   +3
    _____
                                                    6 - 0

2. Men at my work "flirt" with me too much, and sometimes they become too forward and seem to "want more."

    -3   -2   -1   0   +1   +2   +3
    _____
                                                    0 - 6

3. My male co-workers never try to explain away my achievements by saying things like, "She only succeeded because she's a woman."

    -3   -2   -1   0   +1   +2   +3
    _____
                                                    6 - 0

4. At least one male at my company has tried to get me to become sexual with him in spite of me letting him know I did not want that.

    -3   -2   -1   0   +1   +2   +3
    _____
                                                    0 - 6

5. I have had a male superior at my company offer me increased salary or a promotion only if I became sexual with him.

    -3   -2   -1   0   +1   +2   +3
    _____
                                                    0 - 6

SEXUAL DISCRIMINATION SCALE

1. I am able to relate to my male co-workers as both a friend and a respected equal.

   -3   -2   -1   0   +1   +2   +3

   $\overline{\qquad}$
   6 - 0

2. I face a "glass ceiling" at my company that denies me advancement that I have earned simply because I'm a woman.

   -3   -2   -1   0   +1   +2   +3

   $\overline{\qquad}$
   0 - 6

3. My salary and my position are roughly equal to those of male co-workers who have accomplished as much as I have.

   -3   -2   -1   0   +1   +2   +3

   $\overline{\qquad}$
   6 - 0

4. My company offers women good career opportunities because it understands and rewards the unique characteristics and talents that women bring to their jobs.

   -3   -2   -1   0   +1   +2   +3

   $\overline{\qquad}$
   6 - 0

5. Men at this company have trouble viewing women in any way other than as sexual objects who should be appendages to men.

   -3   -2   -1   0   +1   +2   +3

   $\overline{\qquad}$
   0 - 6

BURNOUT SCALE

1. I feel tired and discouraged at the end of most workdays.

   -3   -2   -1   0   +1   +2   +3

   $\overline{\qquad}$
   0 - 6

2. I dread going to work in the mornings.

   -3   -2   -1   0   +1   +2   +3

   $\overline{\qquad}$
   0 - 6

3. I have too many responsibilities at work, and I'm not paid enough for them.

   -3   -2   -1   0   +1   +2   +3

   $\overline{\qquad}$
   0 - 6

4. I enjoy the work I do and feel fulfilled by it.

   -3   -2   -1   0   +1   +2   +3

   $\overline{\qquad}$
   6 - 0

5. I have a lot to look forward to during the rest of my career.

    -3   -2   -1   0   +1   +2   +3

                                                        ___
                                                        6 - 0

WORK-NOT-MEANINGFUL SCALE

1. I feel my own work makes an important contribution to my company's product.

    -3   -2   -1   0   +1   +2   +3

                                                        ___
                                                        6 - 0

2. I don't see the quality of my work being recognized and rewarded by my superiors.

    -3   -2   -1   0   +1   +2   +3

                                                        ___
                                                        0 - 6

3. My employer offers me fair, reasonable, and attractive opportunities for promotion and advancement.

    -3   -2   -1   0   +1   +2   +3

                                                        ___
                                                        6 - 0

4. I have the best possible type of work for my abilities and interests.

    -3   -2   -1   0   +1   +2   +3

                                                        ___
                                                        6 - 0

5. If I had it to do all over again, I would pick a completely different type of career.

    -3   -2   -1   0   +1   +2   +3

                                                        ___
                                                        0 - 6

CONFLICTED WORK RELATIONSHIPS SCALE

1. My friendships with co-workers give me invaluable emotional support and encouragement in my career.

    -3   -2   -1   0   +1   +2   +3

                                                        ___
                                                        6 - 0

2. Some of my co-workers are enemies who try to sabotage me because they think that it will help their careers.

    -3   -2   -1   0   +1   +2   +3

                                                        ___
                                                        0 - 6

3. I have had an important mentor at work who has made a huge difference in my career.

    -3   -2   -1   0   +1   +2   +3

                                                        ___
                                                        6 - 0

4. I can't identify with anyone at my job, so I've ended up as a company "loner" whom co-workers haven't gotten to know.

    -3   -2   -1   0   +1   +2   +3

    0 - 6

5. Although I don't have personal friendships with anyone at work, the respect, sensitivity, and appreciation I receive through working with fellow employees means a great deal to me.

    -3   -2   -1   0   +1   +2   +3

    6 - 0

INADEQUATE SOCIAL SUPPORT SCALE

1. Any time I have an argument or ongoing disagreement with a close friend, it upsets me even when I'm at work and interferes with my work performance.

    -3   -2   -1   0   +1   +2   +3

    0 - 6

2. The social friendships I have outside of work are among the most important relationships I have in my life.

    -3   -2   -1   0   +1   +2   +3

    6 - 0

3. I have had trouble making friends outside of work, and I am often lonely away from the job.

    -3   -2   -1   0   +1   +2   +3

    0 - 6

4. I don't know how I would keep going outside of work without my one closest nonromantic friend.

    -3   -2   -1   0   +1   +2   +3

    0 - 6

5. I have no one outside of my immediate family whom I can turn to for emotional support.

    -3   -2   -1   0   +1   +2   +3

    0 - 6

CONFLICTED SEXUAL RELATIONSHIPS SCALE

1. My love relationship with my mate is the most important ingredient in my present happiness with life. (If you don't have a mate at present, circle "0.")

    -3   -2   -1   0   +1   +2   +3

    6 - 0

2. The loss of my central love relationship with a prior mate severely compromised my ability to work for awhile.

-3   -2   -1   0   +1   +2   +3

0 - 6

3. My mate gives me encouragement and support that has been a key part of my career success. (If you don't have a mate at present, circle "0.")

-3   -2   -1   0   +1   +2   +3

6 - 0

4. My mate and I are experiencing painful relationship conflicts that make it impossible for me to do my best on my job. (If you don't have a mate at present, circle "0.")

-3   -2   -1   0   +1   +2   +3

0 - 6

5. I believe that having a stable love relationship with a dependable mate is essential for being "the best I can be" in my career.

-3   -2   -1   0   +1   +2   +3

0 - 6

CONFLICTED CHILD RELATIONSHIPS SCALE

1. My relationship(s) with my child(ren) has nothing to do with making my life fulfilled and worthwhile. (If you don't have children, circle "0.")

-3   -2   -1   0   +1   +2   +3

0 - 6

2. I experience ongoing conflicts with at least one child of mine that have made me miserable for some time. (If you don't have children, circle "0.")

-3   -2   -1   0   +1   +2   +3

0 - 6

3. My child(ren) believe(s) in me and encourage(s) me in ways that really help me perform better at work. (If you don't have children, circle "0.")

-3   -2   -1   0   +1   +2   +3

6 - 0

4. The time demands and unpredictable problems that are an inevitable part of raising my child(ren) prevent me from doing as well as I could at work. (If you don't have children, circle "0.")

-3   -2   -1   0   +1   +2   +3

0 - 6

5. I believe that having (a) close and loving relationship(s) with my child(ren) is essential for being the "best I can be" in my career. (If you don't have children, circle "0.")

    -3   -2   -1   0   +1   +2   +3

    $\overline{\text{0 - 6}}$

PERFECTIONISTIC SELF-DEMANDS SCALE

1. My self-esteem rises and falls in accordance with how well I'm performing at work and succeeding in relationships.

    -3   -2   -1   0   +1   +2   +3

    $\overline{\text{0 - 6}}$

2. I like myself and enjoy others' company regardless of whether my career is going well or going poorly.

    -3   -2   -1   0   +1   +2   +3

    $\overline{\text{6 - 0}}$

3. I always get upset with myself if I fail to "win," whether it occurs in an important career competition or an unimportant recreational game.

    -3   -2   -1   0   +1   +2   +3

    $\overline{\text{0 - 6}}$

4. I still am able to feel good about myself as a person even if someone I care about is disappointed with me or criticizes my actions.

    -3   -2   -1   0   +1   +2   +3

    $\overline{\text{6 - 0}}$

5. I have been able to "bounce back" from (a) time(s) when I was unable to achieve a major life goal by picking a new goal without "getting down on myself."

    -3   -2   -1   0   +1   +2   +3

    $\overline{\text{6 - 0}}$

PERFORMANCE-DRIVEN PARENTAL
APPROVAL SCALE

1. In spite of all my achievements, I almost never felt both of my parents believed I was "good enough."

    -3   -2   -1   0   +1   +2   +3

    $\overline{\text{0 - 6}}$

2. I always knew that my parents loved and cherished me, even when I made mistakes or failed at something.

    -3   -2   -1   0   +1   +2   +3

                                                       6 - 0

3. I felt like I always had to follow the paths that my parents chose for me, even when they clashed with what I wanted to do.

    -3   -2   -1   0   +1   +2   +3

                                                       0 - 6

4. My parents always encouraged me and supported me in my life choices even if they didn't understand or didn't personally identify with what I was doing.

    -3   -2   -1   0   +1   +2   +3

                                                     6 - 0

5. My parents always believed that you were either a "winner" or a "loser" and that there was "no in-between."

    -3   -2   -1   0   +1   +2   +3

                                                     0 - 6

F
E
S
S

FESS QUESTIONNAIRE SCORING INSTRUCTIONS

To score the FESS Questionnaire, refer to the blank on the far right next to each item, and the two-digit scoring key beneath each blank. Assign a point value for each scoring key as follows:

"6-0" assigns point values to each rating as specified:

> -3 gets a point value of 6
> -2 gets a point value of 5
> -1 gets a point value of 4
> 0 gets a point value of 3
> +1 gets a point value of 2
> +2 gets a point value of 1
> +3 gets a point value of 0

"0-6" assigns point values to each rating as specified:

> -3 gets a point value of 0
> -2 gets a point value of 1
> -1 gets a point value of 2
> 0 gets a point value of 3
> +1 gets a point value of 4
> +2 gets a point value of 5
> +3 gets a point value of 6

Add the five scores together for each scale and enter the total in the corresponding blank for each scale in the following table. To calculate the composite FESS Score, total all the scale scores together and divide this total by ten. To the right of each score, circle the range of scores that contains this score.

Scale Totals		Symptoms Absent	Average Range	Mild Symptoms	Moderate Symptoms	Severe Symptoms
Sexual Harassment	=	0-1	2-12	13-17	18-23	24-30
Sexual Discrimination	=	0-3	4-16	17-22	23-28	29-30
Burnout	=	0	1-15	16-23	24-30	xxxxx
Work-Not-Meaningful	=	0-1	2-14	15-21	22-27	28-30
Conflicted Work Relationships	=	0-1	2-12	13-17	18-22	23-30
Inadequate Social Support	=	0-4	5-14	15-19	20-24	25-30
Conflicted Sexual Relationships	=	0-5	6-14	15-18	19-23	24-30
Conflicted Child Relationships	=	0-7	8-16	17-20	21-24	25-30
Perfectionistic Self-Demands	=	0-6	7-18	19-24	25-30	xxxxx
Performance-Driven Parental Approval	=	0	1-14	15-22	23-29	30
Total of all Ten Scales	=( )					
Divide this total by 10 to produce:						
Composite FESS Score	=	0-5	6-12	13-15	16-19	20-30

Symptoms Absent Range: Suggests significantly less stress in this area than the majority of average women.

Average Range: Suggests stress level in this area that is fairly typical for average women.

Mild Symptoms Range: Suggests some symptoms of stress that may be significant enough to compromise daily functioning but are not strong enough to be debilitating.

Moderate Symptoms Range: Suggests symptoms that may be strong enough to impair adequate functioning and cause brief and sporadic episodes of debilitation.

Severe Symptoms Range: Suggests symptoms that may prevent adequate functioning much of the time and might produce episodic symptoms of depression or anxiety.

FESS

APPENDIX II

FESS study statistical data: What they tell us

FESS Sample vs. Established Norms for All Questionnaires

	FESS Study Sample (N = 87)	POMS Adult Norms (N = 1,230 Females)
Profile of Mood States		
Tension-Anxiety Scale Mean	9.7	12.8
Depression-Dejection Scale Mean	7.0	10.2
Anger-Hostility Scale Mean	8.0	9.7
Vigor-Activity Scale Mean	16.1*	14.9*
Fatigue-Inertia Scale Mean	8.8	8.4
Confusion-Bewilderment Scale Mean	4.7	7.3
Total Mood Disturbance Scale Mean	22.1	33.5**

* Unlike all other POMS scales, health on the Vigor-Activity Scale is indicated by a **higher** score.

** Unweighted mean for this group was not available in the POMS manual. This TMD score reflects the Vigor-Activity mean subtracted from the sum of all the remaining scale means.

	FESS Study Sample (N = 87)	CRI Adult Norms (N = 491 Females)
Coping Resources Inventory		
Cognitive Scale Mean	28.7	27.5
Social Scale Mean	39.6	41.0
Emotional Scale Mean	44.6	47.5
Spiritual/Philosophical Scale Mean	31.3	32.5
Physical Scale Mean	28.1	28.6
Total Score Mean	171.9	177.0

	FESS Study Sample (N = 87)	WCQ Adult Norms (N = 75 Males & 75 Females)
Ways of Coping Questionnaire		
Confrontive Coping Mean	5.2	3.9
Distancing Mean	4.4	3.1
Self-Controlling Mean	10.2	5.8
Seeking Social Support Mean	7.4	5.4

FESS		
Accepting Responsibility Mean	2.9	1.9
Escape-Avoidance Mean	4.2	3.2
Planful Problem-Solving Mean	9.9	7.3
Positive Reappraisal Mean	6.3	3.5

	FESS Study Sample (N = 87) Average Percentile Rank	JAS Adult Norms (N = 2,470 Men) Average Percentile Rank
Jenkins Activity Survey		
Type A Scale	80th percentile	50th percentile
Speed and Impatience Factor	20th percentile	50th percentile
Job Involvement Factor	75th percentile	50th percentile
Hard-Driving and		
Competitive Factor	60th percentile	50th percentile

	FESS Study Sample (N=87)	BSRI Adult Female Norms (N=340)	BSRI Adult Male Norms (N=476)
<u>Bem Sex-Role Inventory</u>			
Femininity Scale			
Mean T-Score	49	54	46
Masculinity Scale			
Mean T-Score	59	48	52
Feminine Classification	9%	39%	12%
Masculine Classification	54%	12%	42%
Androgynous Classification	30%	30%	20%
Undifferentiated Classification	7%	18%	27%

	FESS Study Sample (N = 87)	CSEI Adult Female Norms (N=112)
<u>Coopersmith Self-Esteem Inventory</u>		
Coopersmith SEI Mean Score	84.9	71.6

As a whole, the executives we studied were elite women with tremendous power. And as a group, they were healthier than the rest of society. The above table presents all of the mean (i.e., average) scores for the FESS study sample compared to the test makers' "healthy" average population. When comparing the Profile of Mood States (POMS) scores for our eighty-seven women, a measure of general emotional well-being, to one study of 1,230 adult women, our executives fared better overall. Our sample had healthier average scale scores compared to the other group on all of the POMS scales except Fatigue-Inertia, where the test makers' sample of 1,230 adult women displayed a slightly lower average score. This may suggest that the most pronounced negative mood state of our sample may be fatigue and exhaustion, which would be expected of career women who also have outside family responsibilities.

When comparing the coping skills of our eighty-seven women with the test makers' "healthy" average group of 491 women, we found that average scale scores on the Coping Resources Inventory were very close to the average scores of these other groups. Our sample scored slightly higher on the Cognitive Scale than the other two groups, which suggests that the women in our sample emphasized a self-confident, optimistic, and positive outlook on life. The women in the FESS study achieved slightly lower scores on all of the remaining Coping Resources Inventory scales, but the differences in all cases were small and would not seem to suggest pronounced differences on these scales between the three sample groups.

In contrast to the Coping Resources Inventory comparisons described above, the FESS study sample achieved higher scores than the test makers' "healthy" average sample on all of the Ways of Coping Questionnaire scales. Differences were most pronounced on the Self-Controlling Scale and the Positive Reappraisal Scale, where the average scale scores for the FESS sample were almost double the average scale scores for the test makers' "healthy" sample.

This seems to suggest that our sample emphasized the use of deliberate and calculated efforts to direct and control their emotions and behaviors, and may devote more effort to seek meaningfulness, personal fulfillment, and opportunities for growth in their lives. The Ways of Coping Questionnaire focuses primarily on seven different coping tactics employed in response to a recent stressful event. In contrast, the Coping Resources Inventory addresses everyday thinking-and-feeling patterns, characteristic and general behavioral coping strategies, and routine recreational and health-oriented behavioral patterns that represent basic personality resources for every variety of life situation.

This comparative data may indicate that, although our group as a whole is not remarkably different from adult women in general with regard to basic personality resources, they may have a more varied and developed arsenal of specific and effective behavioral coping tactics that enable them to persevere and succeed in the American workplace.

F
E
S
S

More striking differences emerged on the comparisons of the FESS sample with the test makers' "healthy" average group on the Jenkins Activity Survey. The average score of our sample on the Type A Scale (which measures the general behavior pattern termed "Type A" that has been linked to heart disease in men) was well above the average score for the test makers' "healthy" average sample of 2,470 adult men. In fact, the average Type A score for the FESS sample exceeded the Type A scores for 80 percent of the test makers' "healthy" sample.

The remaining three Jenkins Activity Survey scales measure the three basic components of the Type A behavior pattern that have been discovered by prior research, and the average scale scores of our sample comfortably exceed the average scores of the test makers' "healthy" sample in all three cases.

Clearly the women in the FESS study exhibited pronounced Type A tendencies that exceed the tendencies of the majority of adult working men in America.

The FESS sample displayed patterns on the Bem Sex-Role Inventory that departed from the patterns of the test makers' "healthy" average female sample in several striking ways. Our sample achieved a much higher average score on the Masculinity Scale than on the Femininity Scale, which is the opposite of the pattern produced by the test makers' "healthy" females. Indeed, the masculinity average scale score for the FESS sample was higher than the average score for the test makers' "healthy" male sample as well as their "healthy" female sample.

The Bem Sex-Role Inventory also offers a fourfold classification scheme that characterizes the different forms of sexual role orientation that occur. The following table illustrates this straightforward classification strategy.

BEM SEX-ROLE
INVENTORY CLASSIFICATION SCHEME (Bem, 1981)

		Masculinity Score	
		Below Median	**Above Median**
	Below	Undifferentiated	Masculine
Femininity **Median**		(low-low)	(low fem.-high masc.)
Score			
	Above	Feminine	Androgynous
	Median	(high fem.-low masc.)	(high-high)

F
E
S
S

Using the median scores (i.e., a "T-score" of 51 for the Femininity Scale and a "T-score" of 50 for the Masculinity Scale) to split the range of scores for each scale in half, individual subjects are classified on the basis of being above or below the median for each scale.

For instance, a subject who produced a score below 51 on the Femininity Scale and above 50 on the Masculinity Scale would be classified as masculine. A larger percentage of our sample received the masculine classifications than did the test makers' "healthy" average female and male populations.

Far fewer subjects in our sample were classified as either feminine or undifferentiated than the subjects in the test makers' "healthy" samples, while similar percentages of subjects were classified as androgynous in each sample. It is quite remarkable that our all-female sample received a substantially greater percentage of masculine classifications and a slightly smaller percentage of feminine classifications than the test makers' "healthy" average group of males.

According to the Coopersmith Self-Esteem Inventory, our sample scored substantially higher on self-esteem than the test makers' "healthy" average samples of females only as well as females and males combined. Indeed, our sample's average Coopersmith Self-Esteem Inventory score closely approached the test makers' cutoff score for high self-esteem that was exceeded only by 25 percent of their "healthy" average sample.

What these comparisons tell us is that our sample of women are representative of the larger population of women in this country in several respects. This suggests that it is reasonable to extrapolate information gleaned from them and apply it to everyday use for all women. However, we do realize that there was a selection factor at work, as there is in all research. Our subjects were volunteers asked to participate in a study that would take them well over an hour to complete. The women we were trying to reach were busy executives juggling hectic schedules. We assume that the women who did not complete the packet—the 213 who did not respond—were likely among the most stressed executives and did not want to add another task to their already overly full day. Also, we assume that those who did complete the packet were among the most energetic—those who couldn't stand to leave something so fat in their "in" box before they left for the day.

The 300 packets were sent to a large national retailing company, individual members of the National Association of Female Executives, and a national financial services firm. We had the best cooperation from the national retailing company since the management repeatedly requested their participation.

Understanding the FESS Study Executives

The FESS study provided many clues to why some executives are healthy and successful and others are hindered by stress. Before we decipher their mood states and coping strategies, it's important to understand how these executives think and feel.

The Bem Sex-Role Inventory classifies individuals as "male," "female," "androgynous," and "undifferentiated." While these labels are somewhat misleading and dated, the following selected sample of "male" and "female" characteristics used in the test will give you an idea of what the testers had in mind. Nineties' terminology for the following scales would be "hard" for the Masculine Scale and "soft" for the Feminine Scale. Most of us have a combination of these hard and soft characteristics forming our personality.

Masculine Items— "Hard" (Bem, 1981)	Feminine Items— "Soft" (Bem, 1981)
Forceful	Affectionate
Willing to take risks	Compassionate
Dominant	Love children
Aggressive	Gentle
Self-reliant	Yielding
Athletic	Shy
Analytical	Loyal
Competitive	Gullible
Ambitious	Childlike
Act as a leader	Do not use harsh language

In the Bem Sex-Role Inventory, those who score high on the male side and low on the female side are classified "male," and those who score high on the female side and low on the male side are classified "female." Those who score high on both sides are classified as "androgynous," while those who score low on both sides are classified as "undifferentiated."

Given these definitions, it is not surprising that 55 percent of the FESS study executives were classified as masculine; 7 percent were classified as feminine; 24 percent were classified as androgynous; and 14 percent were classified as undifferentiated. To make it in corporate America, these women have been required to abandon their "soft" sides and embrace their "hard" sides.

Executives and Emotional Distress

To understand how these executives feel about themselves and life in general, we used a Profile of Mood States (POMS) (McNair, Lorr, and Droppleman, 1992) that looked at their overall emotional distress, measuring feelings such as "fatigue-inertia," "anger-hostility," "total mood disturbance," "depression-dejection," "confusion-bewilderment," and "tension-anxiety." The POMS also measured one positive aspect of mood on a scale called "vigor-activity." The POMS scores correlated very highly with several of the scales on the FESS Questionnaire, indicating which problems caused the most emotional distress for the FESS study executives.

The FESS Questionnaire that was created for this study included ten FESS scales and a composite score. The ten scales measured sexual harassment, sexual discrimination, burnout, how meaningful these executives found their work, conflicts in work relationships, problems with social support, problems with sexual relationships, problems with child relationships, perfectionistic self-demands, and performance-driven/parental-approval tendencies. The composite score is the sum of these ten scores divided by ten, basically producing an "average" FESS scale score.

Statistical analyses revealed that six of the FESS Questionnaire scales (i.e., Work-Not-Meaningful, Burnout, Conflicted Work Relationships, Perfectionistic Self-Demands, and the Composite Score) were strongly related to all six of the POMS scales that measured emotional distress. The four POMS scales measuring anxiety, depression, anger, and total mood disturbances were strongly related in the same manner to the Sexual Discrimination Scale and Conflicted Sexual Relationships Scale of the FESS Questionnaire. The remaining FESS Questionnaire scales (i.e., Inadequate Social Support, Sexual Harassment, and Performance-Driven Parental Approval) had very few significant relationships with the POMS scales.

Analyses of the relationships between the POMS scales and the scales from the two coping questionnaires revealed that the Coping Resources Inventory Cognitive Scale and Physical Scale were strongly related to all seven POMS scales. This indicates the possession and employment of these two coping resources substantially reduces all emotional distress symptoms measured by six POMS scales and substantially increases desirable symptoms of energy measured by the POMS Vigor Activity Scale. High scores on the Coping Resources Inventory Cognitive Scale suggest the presence of a positive self-image, a positive outlook toward others, and a general optimism about life. High scores on the Coping Resources Inventory Physical Scale suggest the regular pursuit of exercise, activity, and other health-promoting behaviors.

The possession and employment of two specific coping strategies—confrontive coping and escape avoidance—increased emotional distress in the subjects of this study. High scores on the Ways of Coping Questionnaire Confrontive Coping Scale suggested the use of hostility, taking risks, and aggressive action to cope with a stressful situation, while high scores on the Ways of Coping Questionnaire Escape-Avoidance Scale suggested efforts to retreat and hide from stressful situations by withdrawing into wishful thinking fantasies.

How to cope
We can learn a great deal from these executives about coping. The FESS study discovered a strong relationship between the coping skills in the subjects' behavioral repertoire and their ability to effectively withstand and overcome stress. Problem-focused coping worked best in situations where the outcome could be influenced or controlled, while emotion-focused coping was better in situations not under their control. The most successful women were flexible, able to pick and choose among a wide variety of coping skills. The most distressed women primarily chose to avoid and/or escape from problems, or they were too aggressive and confrontive, and ultimately far less flexible.

APPENDIX III

Solutions to FESS:
An executive woman's survival guide in the corporate American jungle

**COMPARISON OF DEMOGRAPHIC VARIABLES
BETWEEN FESS STUDY GROUPS**

	Seasoned Executives	Young Turks	Stressed Group	Total Sample
Percentage of				
Total Sample	14%	18%	68%	100%
Average Age	44.3 yrs.	39.6 yrs.	42.2 yrs.	42.0 yrs.
Marital Status				
Single, Never Married	8%	6%	12%	10%
Married	92%	69%	63%	68%
Separated/Divorced/Widowed	0%	25%	25%	22%
Number of Children				
None	42%	56%	37%	41%
One	17%	31%	14%	17%
Two	42%	6%	41%	35%
Three to Five	0%	0%	4%	2%
Unspecified, but have children	0%	6%	4%	5%
Average Number of Years				
with Present Company	20.3 yrs.	16.7 yrs.	13.8 yrs.	15.2 yrs.
Level of Yearly Salary				
$75,000 or More	58%	50%	43%	47%
Less than $75,000	42%	50%	57%	53%
Salary Compared to Mate's				
(68 subjects responded)				
I make over				
$10,000 more	92%	58%	52%	61%
I make less than				
$10,000 more	0%	8%	14%	10%

Mate makes less than				
$10,000 more	0%	17%	11%	10%
Mate makes over				
$10,000 more	8%	17%	23%	19%

The above table compares the two healthy groups with the stressed group on several demographic variables. It is remarkable that over 90 percent of the Seasoned Executives are married, while only about two-thirds of the members of the other groups are married. Forty-two percent of this group do not have children, with the remaining 58 percent having one or two children. Fifty-eight percent of the Seasoned Executives make $75,000 or more per year; no more than half of the other two groups have reached this level.

While over 90 percent of the Seasoned Executives have salaries that are $10,000 or more above the salaries of their mates, the other groups have less than 60 percent of their members with mates who fit this comparative salary description. The Seasoned Executives comprise only 14 percent of the overall sample; they appear to be the most successful in their careers as well as in their family roles.

MARITAL RELATIONSHIPS OF THREE GROUPS

	Seasoned Executives	Young Turks	Stressed Group	Total Sample
Marital Satisfaction (73 Subjects Responded)				
Unhappy/Unstable-				
Troubled/OK-Troubled	8%	0%	34%	23%
Satisfied/Happy-				
Fulfilled	92%	100%	66%	77%
Extramarital Affairs (85 Subjects Responded)				
Never Had An Affair	83%	60%	55%	60%
Yes, In The Past	17%	27%	41%	35%
Yes, Currently	0%	13%	4%	5%

The Marital Relationships table above offers more information as to the quality of the marital relationships in the three groups. The Seasoned Executives and the Young Turks both displayed extremely high levels of satisfaction with their present love relationships, while only about two-thirds of the Stressed Group claimed similar levels of satisfaction.

The findings about extramarital affairs were even more striking: 83 percent of the Seasoned Executives claimed they had never had an affair, while only 60 percent of the Young Turks and 55 percent of the Stressed Group made the same claim. Most of the extramarital affairs reported were in the past, although 13 percent of the Young Turks and 4 percent of the Stressed Group were actively involved in extramarital affairs at the time of the study.

The following table describes all of the questionnaire scales displaying significant differences between the three groups. "Highly Significant Differences" identify findings that have no more than one chance out of one hundred of occurring coincidentally. "Marginally Significant Differences" indicate those findings that have no more than one chance out of twenty of such an occurrence. Some researchers would not regard these latter findings as significant due to the high number of total statistical tests conducted for this study.

SIGNIFICANT DIFFERENCES BETWEEN THE THREE GROUPS ON ALL QUESTIONNAIRE SCALES

	Seasoned Executives Average Score	Young Turks Average Score	Stressed Group Average Score	Relevant Established Adult "Healthy" Norms
HIGHLY SIGNIFICANT DIFFERENCES				
Levels of External Stress (FESS Questionnaire)				
Burnout Scale	6.0	4.0	10.4	None Avail.
Work-Not-Meaningful Scale	4.4	5.9	9.8	None Avail.
Conflicted Sexual Relationships Scale	7.7	9.1	11.4	None Avail.
Performance-Driven Parental Approval Scale	4.0	4.1	9.9	None Avail.
Composite FESS Score	6.8	7.1	10.2	None Avail.
Internal Emotional State (Profile of Mood States)				
Depression-Dejection Scale	1.3	3.6	9.1	10.2
Vigor-Activity Scale	22.3*	17.2*	14.6*	14.9*
Fatigue-Inertia Scale	4.0	6.9	10.3	8.4
Confusion-Bewilderment Scale	1.7	3.6	5.6	7.3
Total Mood Disturbance Score	25.5	44.5	63.1	33.5

F
E
S
S

Characteristic Coping Strategies

Coping Resources
    Inventory Social Scale   43.2   38.3   39.2   41.0
Coping Resources
    Inventory Total Score   182.6   175.8   168.7   177.0
Ways of Coping Questionnaire
    Self-Controlling Scale   11.7   7.8   10.6   5.8
Ways of Coping Questionnaire
    Accepting Responsibility Scale 1.9   1.3   3.5   1.9

Stable Personality Traits

Coopersmith Self-Esteem
    Inventory   88.8   90.4   78.0   71.6
Bem Sex-Role Inventory
    Femininity Scale   53.8   43.2   49.2   54.0
Jenkins Activity Survey
    Job Involvement Scale   274.8   289.1   256.6   218.0

MARGINALLY SIGNIFICANT DIFFERENCES

Levels of External Stress (FESS Questionnaire)
Sexual Discrimination Scale   9.1   6.8   11.3None Avail.
Conflicted Work
    Relationships Scale   6.4   8.3   9.5None Avail.

Internal Emotional State (Profile of Mood States)
Tension-Anxiety Scale   7.0   6.1   11.2   12.8
Anger-Hostility Scale   2.8   5.3   9.8   9.7

Characteristic Coping Strategies

Coping Resources
    Inventory Emotional Scale   47.7   45.8   43.6   47.5
Coping Resources
    Inventory Physical Scale   29.0   30.4   27.2   28.6
Ways of Coping Questionnaire
    Confrontive Coping Scale   4.3   3.5   5.8   3.9
Ways of Coping Questionnaire
    Escape-Avoidance Scale   1.8   4.1   4.8   3.2

* Unlike all other POMS scales, health on the Vigor-Activity Scale is indicated by a higher score.

These results indicate that the Seasoned Executives were the most effective at minimizing external stress overall, at work and at home. They had
the lowest average scores on several FESS Questionnaire scales, namely
the Work-Not-Meaningful Scale, the Conflicted Sexual Relationships
Scale, and the Conflicted Work Relationships Scale. They were more
vigorous, energetic, and cheerful than the rest of the sample, and they
displayed the fewest number of emotional distress symptoms. The
Seasoned Executives had the highest average score on the Profile of
Mood States (POMS) Vigor-Activity Scale (the only POMS scale where
the higher score indicates health) and the lowest average score on several other POMS scales, namely the Depression-Dejection Scale, the
Fatigue-Inertia Scale, the Confusion-Bewilderment Scale, the Total
Mood Disturbance Score, and the Anger-Hostility Scale.

Specifically, the Seasoned Executives showed the fewest symptoms of
cognitive confusion, the fewest symptoms of depression, the fewest symptoms of anger, and the fewest symptoms of fatigue. Not only was this
group the healthiest when compared to the rest of the women in the study,
but when compared to society in general. Many of this group's scores were
healthier than the scores for "healthy" populations that the test makers
used as a comparison when they derived the tests.

Coping Skills of the Seasoned Executive

How do the Seasoned Executives cope so well? One of the things they do
more than any other group in the study is seek social involvement with
others, turning to other people when they are stressed and looking for
support. They have regular social involvements. To put it simply, they
have solid groups of friends. Women who suffer from FESS, however, are
deficient in social support and tend to be isolated and more often alone.

The Seasoned Executives pick appropriate ways to release negative
emotions instead of stuffing them. They exert enough self-control to
pick the times and places to vent in ways that will not be harmful to them,
including physical exercise and activity.

Perhaps the most important aspect of their superior coping style is
their flexibility, since they seem to have many different coping strategies
at their disposal and switch easily from one strategy to another to best
respond to the immediate situation. These observations are supported by
the significantly higher (and healthier) average scores of the Seasoned
Executives in comparison with the other study groups and the "healthy"
average populations on several of the Coping Resources Inventory scales
(i.e., the Social Scale, the Total Score, and the Emotional Scale) and a
Ways of Coping Questionnaire scale (i.e., the Self-Controlling Scale).

In addition, while the average score for the Seasoned Executives on the Coping Resources Inventory Physical Activity Scale was not quite as high as the score is for the Young Turks, it was higher than the average score for the Stressed Group and the "healthy" average population.

In other words, the Seasoned Executives are thinkers. They try to think problems through before acting. They exert a great deal of self-control. They are both logical and deliberate when they do decide to take action. They have the ability to regulate and restrain their behavior and their expression of their feelings in accordance with what they think is more adaptive to any given situation. They are focused and intense and introspective in the way they approach their lives. This is their general coping style.

A coping strategy that is characteristically avoided by this group of women is the escape-avoidance strategy, or what you might call "wishful thinking." These women typically reject wishful thinking as a coping response because they do not try to avoid problems. They do not withdraw into fantasy. They are doers. They are effective and confident that they can handle a variety of situations, and they don't shrink from challenge. This is supported by the fact that the Seasoned Executives have the lowest score of all groups on the Ways of Coping Questionnaire Escape-Avoidance Scale.

FESS women who are depressed often find themselves fantasizing about solutions to their problems. They have a feeling of helplessness. They want to change, but believe they are incapable of adapting because they do not respect and value themselves; however, the more they can activate themselves, their confidence, and their self-esteem in therapy, the more they see that they can become "doers." As a result, they rely less on fantasy.

The Seasoned Executives don't let stress disrupt their thinking or stir up their emotional state and throw them into turmoil. They don't permit stress to disrupt their lives. Period. They are firmly in command and show a high level of mastery over their own lives. They are logical and bright and good problem solvers. They are creative and flexible. They can change strategies or tactics depending on the problems they are facing. This fluid flexibility in coping strategies is a crucial part of what makes them so highly adaptable.

The Seasoned Executives displayed the best balance between "feminine" and "masculine" ("soft" and "hard") characteristics of any group in the study. About 83 percent of this group identified more with feminine characteristics than the average American woman, while 100 percent of the group identified more with masculine characteristics than the average American woman. In other words, they had an unusually high emphasis on masculine characteristics and an almost equally strong emphasis on feminine characteristics. With ready access to both their hard and soft sides, these women could utilize a flexible and adaptive coping strategy that best fit their immediate needs.

These findings demonstrate that, at higher corporate levels, you have to rely upon a solid network of social support to control and buffer your stress. You have to exert self-control and keep your wits when the stress is high, and to have the gumption to follow through behaviorally. And when you figure out the solution to a situation, you do something—you follow through.

Adaptive Personality Traits of the Seasoned Executives

One of the most remarkable aspects of both of the healthy groups in this study was their extremely high self-esteem scores. The Seasoned Executives had an average Coopersmith Self-Esteem Inventory score that was not quite as high as the average score for the Young Turks group. However, both of these groups displayed average scores that were substantially higher than the average scores for the Stressed Group and the "healthy" average population utilized by the test makers.

Indeed the average scores for both of the healthy groups in the FESS study exceeded the scaled score of 85 that indicated high self-esteem, a feat accomplished by only 25 percent of the "healthy" average population. Clearly, the Seasoned Executives and the Young Turks both displayed a robust and resilient self-confidence and self-regard that was a central component of their career success.

The Seasoned Executives displayed the highest average score for the Bem Sex-Role Inventory Femininity or "Soft Scale" of all of the groups in this study. Yet their score was virtually identical with the average score of the test makers' "healthy" average female population. Although the average score differences for the Bem Sex-Role Inventory Masculinity, or Hard Scale, were not statistically significant, the average score of the Seasoned Executives (62.8) was slightly higher than the average scores of the Young Turks (61.1) and the Stressed Group (58.1). All of these average scores, however, were substantially higher than the average score for the test makers' "healthy" average female population (48.0).

BEM SEX-ROLE INVENTORY CLASSIFICATIONS
OF THE THREE GROUPS

	Seasoned Executives	Young Turks	Stressed Group	Total Sample	BRSI Adult Female Norms (N=340)	BRSI Adult Male Norms (N=470)
Feminine	0%	0%	14%	9%	39%	12%
Masculine	42%	81%	49%	54%	12%	42%
Androgynous	58%	13%	29%	30%	30%	20%
Undifferentiated	0%	6%	8%	7%	18%	27%

The Seasoned Executives had 58 percent of their members classified as "Androgynous," meaning they possessed high numbers of both male and female characteristics, while none of the other groups had more than 30 percent in this category.

As a whole, all of the executive women we studied produced high scores on the so-called Masculinity or Hard Scale, but the women in the Seasoned Executive group identified with characteristics that could be called "the best of both." They exhibited a balance of soft and hard characteristics that may produce the flexible and adaptive coping strategies that make them successful. One of the study subjects described this as having the flexibility to "think like a man and feel like a woman."

Perhaps most importantly, these study findings show that the characteristics considered "male" are not exclusively male adjectives at all, just as the characteristics from the female column are not exclusively female. But the study shows that the women with the greatest success in corporate America have ready access to both columns, to both extremes of human feeling that were once labeled gender-specific.

A final significant personality trait emerged from the Jenkins Activity Survey Job Involvement Scale. The Young Turks scored the highest, followed by the Seasoned Executives and then the Stressed Group. All three of the FESS study groups, however, displayed much higher average scores than the test makers' "healthy" average group, who, incidentally, were all men.

The Seasoned Executives also displayed the second-lowest average score on the FESS Questionnaire Burnout Scale, with only the Young Turks displaying a lower average score. Although a high level of career involvement (a component of the Type A personality) may contribute to some physical health problems, it seems to be a positive factor for working women.

Stress and the Young Turks

Test results indicate that this group displayed more signs of overall emotional stress than the Seasoned Executives, but they showed less distress than the remaining subjects. The Profile of Mood States scores placed the Young Turks in the middle of scales that measure vigor, activity, and energy, just below the Seasoned Executives. For confusion, depression, anxiety, anger, and fatigue, they were literally halfway between the healthiest group and the rest of the subjects. Basically, these women are more successful than most at dealing with emotional distress, just not quite as effective as the Seasoned Executives.

In terms of defensive strategies, the Young Turks did utilize the escape and avoidance strategies in problem solving that the Seasoned Executives avoided, using these strategies almost as much as the remaining women in the study. They had a tendency to deny problems and navigate around them rather than confronting them. This is indicated by the average score for the Young Turks on the Ways of Coping Questionnaire's Escape-Avoidance Scale, which was higher than the average scores of the Seasoned Executives and the test makers' "healthy" average group, but was not quite as high as the average score of the Stressed Group.

They did not rely upon social involvement and support at all. In fact, they were less likely to turn to a social network than the women in the Stressed Group, as is indicated by their lower average scores on the Coping Resources Inventory Social Scale as compared to the two other groups in the study and the test makers' "healthy" average group. In other words, they were the least social of all of the women studied. They were more impulsive and emotional than the Seasoned Executives; however, they still were far less stressed than the Stressed Group.

Adaptive Personality Traits of the Young Turks

The Young Turks achieved the highest average Coopersmith Self-Esteem Inventory score of all four groups, as shown in the chart on page 208. As mentioned earlier, their average score of 90.4 comfortably exceeded the cutoff score of 85, designated as the minimum score indicating the presence of high self-esteem. The Young Turks' exceptional self-esteem is crucial to their success.

The Young Turks were the most "masculine" group in the entire sample, producing the lowest average score on the Bem Sex-Role Inventory Femininity Scale of 43.2 and the highest on the Masculinity Scale at 61.1. Almost 88 percent of this group identified less with feminine characteristics than the average American woman, while about 94 percent of this group identified more with masculine characteristics than the average American woman.

This difference is dramatized by the Bem Sex-Role Inventory classifications for each group that are in the table on page 212. The astonishing 81 percent of the Young Turks classified as masculine towers above these percentages for all other groups described by the table—even dwarfing the 42 percent masculine classifications observed in the test makers' "healthy" average male population.

In spite of their strengths and ability to deal with stress, the Young Turks are not in touch with their femininity, or soft side. This lack of flexibility prohibits them from employing the adaptive coping style typical of the Seasoned Executives, who are able to rely on the best of both sides. The Young Turks experience far more stress with fellow workers than the Seasoned Executives, partly due to their single-mindedness and their inability to be flexible in their coping responses.

The remaining significant personality trait emerged in the average scores of the groups on the Jenkins Activity Survey Job Involvement Scale. The Young Turks had the highest average score of all of the groups in the study. As mentioned earlier, all of our study groups had substantially higher scores than the test makers' all-male "healthy" average group. A related finding was the Young Turks' lowest average score on the FESS Questionnaire Burnout Scale of all three study groups. The Young Turks seemed to be highly involved, highly committed, and still quite excited in regard to their careers.

Why are they so successful? They are completely focused and entirely driven. They are single minded in their approach to business. They are rigidly locked into the personality style that is now popularly called "Type A." These women are the most hard driving, the most ambitious, and the most energized of any of the women in the study.

The Young Turks have their obsessive defenses down solid. They are goal oriented and highly focused on work. They can detach themselves from the stresses or problems at hand and get the job done, in contrast to those in the Stressed Group who have far more leaks in their defense systems.

F
E
S
S

In essence, this group is more successful at minimizing stress than most of the population, though less successful than the Seasoned Executives. The trouble they have accessing their soft side seems to produce a more rigid, "masculine" or hard coping style that is less successful than the more flexible, well-rounded style exhibited by the Seasoned Executives.

The Road to Success

The two successful groups, the Seasoned Executives and the Young Turks, were statistically very similar to each other. When these two successful groups were combined into one group in the statistical analyses, they were significantly different from the rest of the sample as the table below shows.

SIGNIFICANT DIFFERENCES BETWEEN THE SEASONED EXECUTIVES AND THE YOUNG TURKS TREATED AS ONE GROUP VS. THE STRESSED GROUP

	Healthy Executives Average	Stressed Group Average
HIGHLY SIGNIFICANT DIFFERENCES		
Levels of External Stress (FESS Questionnaire)		
Burnout Scale	4.9	10.4
Work-Not-Meaningful Scale	5.3	9.8
Sexual Discrimination Scale	7.8	11.3
Conflicted Sexual Relations Scale	8.5	11.4
Performance-Driven Parental Approval Scale	4.0	9.9
Composite Score	7.0	10.2
Internal Emotional State (Profile of Mood States)		
Tension-Anxiety Scale	6.6	11.2
Depression-Dejection Scale	2.6	9.1
Anger-Hostility Scale	4.3	9.8
Vigor-Activity Scale	19.4*	14.6*
Fatigue-Inertia Scale	5.6	10.3
Confusion-Bewilderment Scale	2.8	5.6
Total Mood Disturbance Score	4.4	31.1

F
E
S
S

Characteristic Coping Strategies
Coping Resources
> Inventory Emotional Scale   46.6   43.6

Coping Resources
> Inventory Total Score   178.7   168.7

Ways of Coping Questionnaire
> Accepting Responsibility Scale   1.6   3.5

Stable Personality Traits
Coopersmith Self-Esteem Inventory   89.6   78.0

Jenkins Activity Survey Job
> Involvement Scale   282.9   256.6

MARGINALLY SIGNIFICANT DIFFERENCES
Levels of External Stress (FESS Questionnaire)
Conflicted Work Relationships Scale   7.5   9.5

Perfectionistic Self-Demands Scale   10.6   13.8

Characteristic Coping Strategies
Coping Resources
> Inventory Cognitive Scale   30.0   28.2

Coping Resources Inventory
> Physical Scale   29.8   27.3

Ways of Coping Questionnaire
> Confrontive Coping Scale   3.8   5.8

Stable Personality Traits
BEM SRI Femininity Scale   115.5   108.2

Demographic Variables
Number of Years
> Employed by Present Co.   18.2   13.8

* Unlike all other POMS scales, health on the Vigor-Activity Scale is indicated by a **higher** score.

The Stressed Group, comprising the remaining 68 percent of the FESS study, suffered far more distress than the pooled combination of the two healthy groups, hereinafter referred to as the "Healthy Executives." When we measured for self-esteem, the Healthy Executives exhibited far higher self-esteem scores, which had a direct correlation to their general mental health. Similarly, the Stressed Group had lower self-esteem scores, which directly related to their problems with stress.

When measuring for emotional distress through the Profile of Mood States scales, the Healthy Executives had very low scores, while the Stressed Group reported far more emotional distress of every variety. Because the self-esteem scores so directly related to these feelings, it seems that the Healthy Executives buffered stress with high self-esteem. Their defenses were generally more efficient than those for the Stressed Group.

When measuring for job commitment with the Jenkins Activity Survey Job Involvement Scale, the Healthy Executives showed a much higher level of involvement in their jobs than the remaining subjects. This result also indicated that being truly invested in their work acted as a stress buffer for them.

Another area of great difference was in coping styles. The average scores on the Ways of Coping Questionnaire Accepting Responsibility Scale showed that the Stressed Group had a far greater tendency to accept responsibility for problems as a way of coping with them. They tried to fix everything themselves, and were far more apt to see themselves as a part of the problem. The average scores on the Ways of Coping Questionnaire Confrontive Coping Scale suggested that they may have tried to fix things with confrontations characterized by excessive aggression, hostility, and risk taking. Here again, the Healthy Executives used self-esteem, adaptive releasing of negative emotions, physical exercise, and coping flexibility as important survival skills. These conclusions are supported by the higher average scores for the Healthy Executives on the Coopersmith Self-Esteem Inventory Emotional Scale, the Coping Resources Inventory total score, the Coping Resources Inventory Cognitive Scale, and the Coping Resources Inventory Physical Scale.

In a patriarchal working environment where executive women are one down on the totem pole, they can't allow themselves to fall into harmful patterns of taking blame for every problem that comes along and attacking that problem impulsively and aggressively. By doing so, they cut themselves off from the variety of creative solutions that are found through more flexible coping styles.

Beating Burnout

Burnout was another area where the Stressed Group suffered, averaging a burnout score of 10.4 as compared to the Healthy Executives' score of 4.9. Since they have been in the workforce longer than the Stressed Group, you might expect the Healthy Executives to have a higher burnout score. This surprising difference shows just how well they handle stress.

The lower average score of the Healthy Executives on the FESS Sexual Discrimination Scale indicates either the Healthy Executives have encountered less sexual discrimination than the Stressed Group, or they have coped with sexual discrimination more successfully and have not let it distress them as much. In addition, the lower average score on the FESS Questionnaire Work-Not-Meaningful Scale for the Healthy Executives indicates that they found their work far more meaningful than did those women in the Stressed Group. Feeling fulfilled in their work was another important stress buffer for the Healthy Executives. And work-related stress caused more problems for the Stressed Group in their personal lives than it did for the Healthy Executives, as indicated by their scores on the FESS Questionnaire scales measuring problems with sexual relationships.

The Stressed Group proved to exhibit yet another FESS characteristic in their relationships with their parents. They scored high on the scale that indicates parents loved and rewarded them when they performed well but rejected them when they did not perform well. In contrast, the average score for the Healthy Executives was far lower. This score relates directly to self-esteem. While the Stressed Group can't claim that they were loved unconditionally as children, many of the Healthy Executives can. Unconditional parental love generally contributes to a more cohesive and positive self-image as an adult.

Overall, the Healthy Executives had a lower FESS Questionnaire composite score than the Stressed Group, indicating they were far better at managing and dealing with stress. The Healthy Executives were better able to negotiate and solve their problems, and were better at keeping these problems from impacting all areas of their lives.

Integrating Coping Skills
The Stressed Group did not exhibit many of the coping characteristics the Healthy Executives used as a buffer against stress. Being able to accept and express a range of emotions at the appropriate times, being able to cry when sad, for instance, is believed to be an important key to dealing with stress. While the Healthy Executives could express a wide range of emotions, the Stressed Group could not. This further highlights the adaptive coping skills of the Healthy Executives when compared to the rest of the executive women in the study.

The Healthy Executives exhibited a higher level of physical activity than the Stressed Group. Physical activity not only is believed to decrease the level of negative response to stress, but enables a faster recovery from stressful episodes.

A coping skill that the Healthy Executives avoided but the Stressed Group used was aggressive, abrasive confrontation. The Confrontive Coping Scale measures aggressive efforts to alter problematic situations and suggests some degree of hostility and risk taking. Here again, the flexibility and adaptability of the Healthy Executives helped them avoid destructive coping behaviors. The Stressed Group, however, was impulsive and showed a tendency to act first and think later. The Healthy Executives were more calculating and, as a result, more successful.

Overall, the FESS study reveals that executive women function at dramatically different levels psychologically. The Seasoned Executives offer us a picture of working women in full bloom. They have it all—a sense of self that is rich and cohesive—and they know it. They are fully evolved women, both internally and externally.

The Young Turks are a work in progress. They are sitting firmly in the saddle but need to learn that flexibility, intuition, and a strong awareness of one's internal life are valuable assets in the corporate world. They have some things to learn but are on the right path.

The Stressed Group presents a variegated view of the challenges facing executive women. As with the Young Turks, and many of us, they have yet to fully integrate their intellectual and emotional sides to reach maximum effectiveness. They are far more vulnerable to stress because they do not utilize the good coping skills of the Young Turks or the superior strategies of the Seasoned Executives. It is fair to conclude that this group, as contrasted to the Seasoned Executives and the Young Turks, have the most psychological work yet to do. The Stressed Group may be representative of the executive women who struggle the most in the American patriarchy. And they are still learning, evolving, and searching for improved strategies for coping in a man's world.

RESOURCES

Amatea, E. S., and M. L. Fong. "The Impact of Role Stressors and Personal Resources on the Stress Experience of Professional Women." *Psychology of Women Quarterly* 15 (1991): 419-430.

Bedeian, A. G., B. G. Burke, and R. G. Moffett. "Outcomes of work-family conflict among married male and female professionals." *Journal of Management* 14 (3): 475-491 (1988).

Bem, S. L. *Bem Sex-Role Inventory Professional Manual.* Palo Alto, Calif.: Consulting Psychologists Press, 1981.

Brown, L. M. and C. Gilligan. *Meeting at the Crossroads, Womens' Psychology and Girls' Development.* Cambridge, Mass.: Harvard University Press, 1992.

Burke, R. J., and E. R. Greenglass. "Psychological burnout among men and women in teaching: An examination of the Cherniss model." *Human Relations* 42 (3): 261-273 (1989).

Burnett, J. J., S. D. Hunt, and L. B. Chonko. "Machiavellianism across sexes: An examination of marketing professionals." *Psychological Reports* 59 (1986): 991-994.

Chusmir, L. H. "Gender differences in variables affecting job commitment among working men and women." *The Journal of Social Psychology* 126 (1): 87-94 (1986).

Coleman, J. C. , C. G. Morris, and A. G. Glaros. *Contemporary Psychology and Effective Behavior.* Glenview, Ill.: Scott, Foresman, 1987.

Coopersmith, S. *Self-Esteem Inventories Manual.* Palo Alto, Calif.: Consulting Psychologists Press, 1981.

Crabbs, M. A., K. U. Black, and S. P. Morton. "Stress at work: A comparison of men and women." *Journal of Employment Counseling* 23 (1): 2-8 (1986).

DeMeis, D. K., E. Hock, and S. L. McBride. "The balance of employment and motherhood: Longitudinal study of mothers' feelings about separation from their first-born infants." *Developmental Psychology* 22 (5): 627-632 (1986).

DiSalvo, V., C. Lubbers, A. M. Rossi, and J. Lewis. "The impact of gender on work-related stress." *Journal of Social Behavior and Personality* 3 (3): 161-176 (1988).

Dolan, S. L., and S. Renaud. "Individual, organizational, and social determinants of managerial burnout: A multivariate approach." *Journal of Social Behavior and Personality* 7 (1): 95-110 (1992).

Driscoll, D., and C. R. Goldberg. *Members of the Club - The Coming of Age of Executive Women.* New York, N.Y.: Free Press, 1993.

Eichinger, J., L. J. Heifetz, and C. Ingraham. "Situational shifts in sex role orientation: Correlates of work satisfaction and burnout among women in special education." *Sex Roles* 25 (7/8): 425-440 (1991).

Faludi, S. *Backlash.* New York, N.Y.: Crown, 1991.

Folkman, S., and R. S. Lazarus. *Manual for The Ways of Coping Questionnaire, Research Edition.* Palo Alto, Calif.: Consulting Psychologists Press, 1988.

Fong, M. L., and E. S. Amatea. "Stress and single professional women: An exploration of causal factors." *Journal of Mental Health Counseling* 14 (1): 20-29 (1992).

Friedan, B. *The Feminine Mystique.* London, England: Penguin Books, 1982.

Gable, M., and M. T. Topol. "Machiavellianism and the department store executive." *Journal of Retailing* 64 (1): 68-84 (1988).

Gilligan, C. *In a Different Voice.* Cambridge, Mass.: Harvard University Press, 1982.

Greenglass, E. R. "Burnout and gender: Theoretical and organizational implications." *Canadian Psychology* 32 (4): 562-574 (1991).

Greenglass, E. R., K. Pantony, and R. J. Burke. "A gender-role perspective on role conflict, work stress, and social support." *Journal of Social Behavior and Personality* 3 (4): 317-328 (1988).

Hammer, A. L., and M. S. Marting. *Manual for The Coping Resources Inventory.* Palo Alto, Calif.: Consulting Psychologists Press, 1988.

Henry, S. *The Deep Divide, Why American Women Resist Equality.* New York, N.Y.: MacMillan, 1994.

Hochschild, A. *The Second Shift.* New York, NY: Avon Books, 1989.

Hoff-Sommers, C. *Who Stole Feminism?* New York, N.Y.: Simon & Schuster, 1994.

Holt, P., M. J. Fine, and N. Tollefson. "Mediating stress: Survival of the hardy." *Psychology in the Schools* 24 (1): 51-58, (1987).

Jenkins, C. D., S. J. Zyzanski, and R. H. Rosenman. *Jenkins Activity Survey (Form C)Manual.* San Antonio, Tex.: The Psychological Corporation, 1979.

Kalleberg, A. L., and K. T. Leicht. "Gender and organizational performance: Determinants of small business survival and success." *Academy of Management Journal* 34 (1): 136-161 (1991).

Kessler-Harris, A. *Women Have Always Worked.* New York, N.Y.: Feminist Press, 1981.

King, A. C., and R. A. Winett. "Tailoring stress-reduction strategies to populations at risk: Comparisons between women from dual-career and dual-worker families." *Family and Community Health* 9 (3): 42-50 (1986).

Knight, E. A. "Perceived control and actual outcomes of hassle situations on the job." *Psychological Reports* 67 (3, Pt. 1): 891-898 (1990).

Lobel, S. A., and L. St. Clair. "Effects of family responsibilities, gender, and career identity salience on performance outcomes." *Academy of Management Journal* 35 (5): 1057-1069 (1992).

Long, B. C. "Work-related stress and coping strategies of professional women." *Journal of Employment Counseling* 25 (1): 37-44 (1988).

Long, B. C., S. E. Kahn, and R. W. Schultz. "Causal model of stress and coping: Women in management." *Journal of Counseling Psychology* 39 (2): 227-239 (1992).

McDonald, L. M., and K. Korabik. "Sources of stress and ways of coping among male and female managers." *Journal of Social Behavior and Personality* 6 (7): 185-198 (1991).

McNair, D. M., M. Lorr, and L. F. Droppleman. *EDITS Manual for The Profile of Mood States.* San Diego, Calif.: Educational and Industrial Testing Service, 1992.

Manning, M. R., R. F. Williams, and D. M. Wolfe. "Hardiness and the relationship between stressors and outcomes." *Work and Stress* 2 (3): 205-216 (1988).

Miller, J. G., and K. G. Wheeler. "Unraveling the mysteries of gender differences in intentions to leave the organization." *Journal of Organizational Behavior* 13 (5): 465-478 (1992).

Nelson, D. L., J. C. Quick, and M. A. Hitt. "Men and women of the personnel profession: Some differences and similarities in their stress." *Stress Medicine* 5 (3): 145-152 (1989).

Ogus, E. D., E. R. Greenglass, and R. J. Burke. "Gender-role differences, work stress, and depersonalization." *Journal of Social Behavior and Personality* 5 (5): 387-398 (1990).

Parkes, K. R. "Coping, negative affectivity, and the work environment: Additive and interactive predictors of mental health." *Journal of Applied Psychology* 75 (4): 399-409 (1990).

F
E
S
S

Pretty, G. M. H., M. E. McCarthy, and V. M. Catano. "Psychological environments and burnout: Gender considerations within the corporation." *Journal of Organizational Behavior* 13 (7): 701-711 (1992).

Russo, N. F., R. M. Kelly, and M. Deacon. "Gender and success-related attributions: Beyond individualistic conceptions of achievement." *Sex Roles* 25 (5/6): 331-350 (1991).

Sadker, D., and M. Sadker. *Failing in Fairness - How America's Schools Cheat Girls.* New York, N.Y.: Scribners, 1994.

Steffy, B. D., and D. Ashbaugh. "Dual-career planning, marital satisfaction and job stress among women in dual-career marriages." *Journal of Business and Psychology* 1 (2): 114-123 (1986).

Steinem, G., *Moving Beyond Words.* New York, N.Y.: Simon & Schuster, 1994.

Tavris, C. *The Mismeasure of Women.* New York, N.Y.: Touchstone of Simon & Schuster, 1992.

Tetrick, L. E. and J. M. LaRocco. "Understanding, prediction, and control as moderators of the relationships between perceived stress, satisfaction, and psychological well-being." *Journal of Applied Psychology* 72 (4): 538-543 (1987).

Watkins, S. A. *Introducing Feminism.* National Book, 1994.

Wolf, N. *Fire With Fire.* New York, N.Y.: Random House, 1993.

Working Woman. July, 1994.

INDEX